Hypnosis and NLP
2 Manuscripts

Featuring NLP 2.0 and Hypnosis - How to Hypnotize Anyone

Hypnosis and NLP 2 Manuscripts

Featuring NLP 2.0 and Hypnosis - How to Hypnotize Anyone

The Ultimate Guide to Neuro Linguistic Programming Training, Hypnotherapy, and Real Hypnotism

Hypnosis and NLP Bundle

Published by CAC Publishing LLC.

ISBN 978-1-950010-15-8 paperback
ISBN 978-1-950010-14-1 eBook

The following books are reproduced below with the goal of providing information that is as accurate and reliable as possible. Regardless, purchasing this book can be seen as consent to the fact that both the publisher and the author of this book are in no way experts on the topics discussed within and that any recommendations or suggestions that are made herein are for entertainment purposes only. Professionals should be consulted as needed prior to undertaking any of the actions endorsed herein.

This declaration is deemed fair and valid by both the American Bar Association and the Committee of Publishers Association and is legally binding throughout the United States.

Furthermore, the transmission, duplication or reproduction of any of the following work including specific information will be considered an illegal act irrespective of if it is done electronically or in print. This extends to creating a secondary or tertiary copy of the work or a recorded copy and is only allowed with an expressed written consent from the Publisher. All additional rights reserved.

The information in the following pages is broadly considered to be a truthful and accurate account of facts, and as such any inattention, use or misuse of the information in question by the reader will render any resulting actions solely under their purview. There are no scenarios in which the publisher or the original author of this work can be in any fashion deemed liable for any hardship or damages that may befall them after undertaking information described herein.

Additionally, the information in the following pages is intended only for informational purposes and should thus be thought of as universal. As befitting its nature, it is presented without assurance regarding its prolonged validity or interim quality. Trademarks that are mentioned are done without written consent and can in no way be considered an endorsement from the trademark holder.

Table of Contents

Hypnosis: How to Hypnotize Anyone

The Beginner's Guide to Hypnotism

Hypnosis: How to Hypnotize Anyone

The Beginner's Guide to Hypnotism

Includes the History of Hypnosis, How Hypnotism Works, The Dark Side of Hypnosis, and How to Hypnotize Anyone, Anywhere, Anytime

Kyle Faber

Hypnosis: How to Hypnotize Anyone

The Beginner's Guide to Hypnotism

Published by CAC Publishing LLC.
ISBN 978-1-950010-11-0 paperback
ISBN 978-1-950010-10-3 eBook

Introduction

Congratulations on getting your copy of *Hypnosis: How to Hypnotize Anyone (The Beginner's Guide to Hypnotism)* and thank you for doing so. I know that you will be very pleased with the results and knowledge you will learn from this manual.

The following chapters will discuss:

The history of hypnotism throughout the ages, and famous people involved with hypnotism. The founder of Hypnotism and his amazing discovery will be researched to the fullest extent possible within the scope of this book.

You will learn what the definition of hypnosis is and how it has been defined in the past, as well as the depth and scope of hypnotism. When you are finished reading the chapter on the definition of hypnotism, you might already be very well versed in hypnotism.

We will explore the dark side of how hypnotism is used nefariously by our government, and other governments, to get what they need from people and how they convince people to give up rights and freedoms with hypnotism. You will be provided, of course, with real-life examples of this.

You will learn everything you need to know about hypnotism as far as your gaze, speech, body movements, and directional interaction for an effective hypnotic interview and pre-talk before the subject is put under a trance.

You will learn the full process of trance work. Trance work is a four-part process that uses your fixed focus ability and certain persuasive breathing techniques. This will keep you and the subject both relaxed and will provide you laser beam focus in order to accomplish your hypnotic tasks.

You will be taught the three very different types of hypnotic induction in this tome. The first goes by the name of the relaxation induction. It's where a person is slowly relaxed into a hypnotic state. The second technique is called the confusion induction when a subject's mind is confused into falling into a hypnotic slumber; it is based on a method called apposition of opposites. And finally, a powerful induction technique known as the shock method of induction which involves 8 different points.

Several different trance deepeners will be introduced so that you may bring a hypnotic subject deeper into a hypnotic suggestion. A deeper trance is needed in some hypnotic techniques you will be practicing in this book and in your hypnotic endeavors, so it is an essential skill to master. These powerful states will be achieved by using a means of a directional language of time and space. It may sound a bit deep, but it will be explained in layman's terms that any person will soon be a wizard at using.

Last, you will learn the art of hypnotizing anyone, anywhere and anytime. You will amaze your friends, family and co-workers, and maybe even their families! What you learn will possibly even improve your life and the lives of the people around you. You can use this knowledge to get ahead in your chosen profession or competitive hobby. The possibilities are endless.

There are plenty of books on this subject on the market, so thanks again for choosing this one! Every effort was made to ensure it is full of as much useful information as possible, please enjoy with our sincere best wishes!

Chapter 1: History of Hypnosis

"Many early practices of hypnosis were linked with a belief in religion, magic, and occult," (Bryant 2006: 14). Hypnosis has been used throughout the history of mankind—From early primitive people to the Ancient Egyptians and Greeks to the Australian Aborigines, and even North American Indian medicine men practiced one form of hypnosis or another, (Hathaway. 2003: 2)

The very first kind of hypnotism was something called "Temple Sleep'. Ancient peoples that had something troubling on their minds would go to their faith house or temple of worship to implore their god or gods to send them a divine message or solution to their particular dilemma. This sort of technique was achieved by putting one's self into a very deep self-hypnotic state that would then lead to powerful dreams that would reveal the solution to the problems that were troubling them.

Avicenna Ibn Sina, a very early Persian Psychologist and Doctor, in his book that goes by the name of "The book of healing" describes using hypnotic techniques in his medical practice and research. He referred to hypnotism in Arabic as "al-wahm al imil" and stated that it is possible to control another person's psyche creating conditions wherein the other person accepts the reality of the hypnotic trance.

Hypnotism has its base roots in two different practices known respectfully as Magnetism and Mesmerism.

A Swiss researcher by the name of Paracelsus who lived in the 14th century was the very first person to practice the strange art of using magnets in combination with a deep trance state to help cure various ailments. He would take the magnet and pass it over the part of the body that was ill or even the whole body, in some cases.

Then he would use his powerful incantations to bring the patient into a trance, and in a great many of the cases, the patient was indeed cured.

Valentine Greatrakes, an Irish lay preacher, would roam around England in the 16th century. He was reported to be able to do his laying on of hands by touching people afflicted with various mental and physical ailments. He would say a few key words and stare into their eyes, and people were miraculously cured. A modern skeptic and well-known stage magician by the name of "The Great Randy" called his healing ability into question. He believed that many of the so-called miracles were, in fact, nothing more than psychosomatic illnesses that were cured by Valentines healing touch and his power of suggestion. He was known to his contemporaries as "The "Stroker" because his hypnotic and pseudo-medical routine was to gently stroke the limb or area on the body that was aching to bring the person back to good health and renewed stamina.

In 1771, a fellow with the unusual moniker of "Father Maximillian Hell" started using hypnosis. He would practice his trade and vocation by placing large magnets on the prone bodies of his students and patients. In 1750, it had been discovered that magnets could be created by simply rubbing iron or steel which really had a lot to do with the explosion of practitioners of hypnotism and magnetism around this time. What was special about Father Hell is that one of his pupils was a young person by the name of Anton Mesmer. Anton Mesmer is considered to be the father of hypnotic suggestion.

Franz Anton Mesmer is a name that is synonymous with hypnotism. He was the man that brought hypnotism to the western scientists of the time. Mesmer was studying "Animal Magnetism" or "Mesmerism" That's a term that is still to this very day, used in terms of speaking of hypnotism. The stories of the time about his wild sessions are pretty strange. For example; the room would be richly decorated with the finest of everything. He had the finest draperies, and the finest mirrors with the most terrific gleam! Gold objects and silver were placed around the sitting room to purposely draw the eye. The light from the candles and censors were always kept at a very low glow, causing a dusk or early morning atmosphere in the working chamber. The rank odor of incense wafted through the closed room intoxicating the participators and spectators alike and causing a light-colored fog to engulf the room. Mesmer would dress up in a flamboyant silk robe, like Joseph's coat of many colors, which had every color in the rainbow embedded in its texture. He would wear a tall pointed cap and carry around a metal rod just as you might expect an ancient wizard would wear. Strange melodies and eerie sounds filled the air courtesy of a bizarre instrument known as a "Glass Harmonica." The gathered would be seated around a large table and made to hold hands, all the time receiving the robust vibrational waves Mr. Mesner was sending out to them with his deep piercing gaze. The problem, however, was that Mesmer was giving private lessons to his female clients causing him to fall into disrepute and scandal. Franz Anton Mesmer died a penniless man in Austria in 1815.

The very first account of a hypnotic trance state being used to anesthetize patients undergoing surgery was a doctor known as Récaimer who put his people under hypnosis in order to painlessly operate on them. Carl Reichenbach was very interested in Récaimer's process and researched it himself to learn more. Many people at that time believed that Récaimer possessed occulted magic powers. Reichenbach did not follow that belief though. He believed it was a power called "Odic Force" after the Norse God, Odin. The scientific community at the time proclaimed this theory to be total bunk and in fact an all-out fabrication, and stated that it was "at best" a pseudo-science.

James Esdaile is reported to have performed 345 major operations while using a form of hypnotism to painlessly cut and prod his patients. He also had a strange way of conducting his sessions and surgeries much like the good Mr. Mesner. He would have the patients lie down on a table, fully prone, and dressed in only the tiniest of loincloths. He would then, like many practitioners, run his hands over the ill person from top of the head to the bottom of the feet. However, Esdaile would form his hands into almost claw-like position when performing the circuit of movements.

During the Civil War in the U.S., hypnotism was used extensively on the battlefield, and was the largest use of hypnotism to treat pain up to that point in time. In time, however, ether was introduced to the battlefield medics, and doctors and hypnotism fell out of use.

During the First World War, hypnotism came back in vogue and was used to treat victims of what was called shellshock, later to be called PTSD. Hypnotism is making another comeback in the field of medicine and psychology to treat many veteran sufferers of PTSD from the modern battlefield. Hypnotism is a big part of the veteran rehabilitation program in today's Army. Deep breathing exercises, cognitive behavioral therapy, and self-hypnosis are all effective tools to help beat depressive and anxiety symptoms, both of which are a huge part of PTSD.

Hypnotism and hypnotists are now accepted by the AMA (American Medical Association) and many other medical bodies across the world, and are a welcome part of rehabilitation for veterans along with physical rehabilitation.

Chapter 2: Definition of Hypnotism

The dictionary defines hypnotism as **"the induction of a state of consciousness in which a person apparently loses the power of voluntary action and is highly responsive to suggestion or direction."**

Here is another acceptable source of information from the respected work," Black's law dictionary. " Hypnotism is **"a psychic or mental state rendering the patient susceptible to suggestion at the will of another." "The hypnotic state is an abnormal condition of the mind and senses, in the nature of trance, artificial catalepsy, or somnambulism, induced in one person by another, by concentration of the attention, a strong effort of volition, and perhaps the exercise of telepathic power not as yet fully understood, or by mental suggestion, in which the condition the**

mental processes of the subject and to a great extent his will are subjugated and directed by those of the operator". Wow, that's a mouthful!

Hypnosis is a special process wherein a man or woman allow themselves to be placed in a highly suggestible state of mind. They may undergo changes such as perception, sense of time, thoughts, and even behaviors by doing things that they never thought that they would do otherwise. For instance, thinking that you're driving in a speeding car and you get pulled over by the police causing you to break into tears. Or that you are super-hot and need to remove your clothes to find cooling comfort, or even get on all fours and bark like a dog.

There are several different types of hypnotic inductions, but the main components are deep concentration and focused attention. A person has to be a bit open to hypnotic suggestion for it to work. A person who steadfastly refuses to follow the required inductions out of stubbornness or a desire to call the hypnotist's bluff will most likely not fall under hypnotic suggestions. No person is un-hypnotizable; however you do have to follow the hypnotic practitioners' instructions to fall into the trance state. Most people have an understanding of hypnotism that comes from television and movies, which is a poor representation of the real process of hypnosis.

Contrary to popular belief, being hypnotized does not cause you to lose control of your behavior or cause you to do anything out of character, such as robbing a bank or committing murder, no matter what television detective stories would have you believe. A hypnotized individual will remain aware of whom and where they are, and unless specifically suggested otherwise, they will probably remember the hypnotic session. That is, unless that particular person is a "somnambulist" or a person that goes into a very deep trance effortlessly. A person like that might not remember the hypnotic session.

When people are hypnotized, they could be said to enter into a hypnotic state. In this state, a person's focus is so deep that they might not notice or be aware of what's going on around them. When people are hypnotized properly, they are highly open to suggestions and other commands. A hypnotized person may feel super relaxed and focused, and they will certainly be much more suggestible.

Most people do not know that hypnotism is a naturally occurring phenomenon. We go in and out of hypnotic states every day, often many times a day. Have you ever been hypnotized by the highway or road to the extent that you arrived at an old address or you weren't able to remember how you somewhere once you got there? You were in a small self-induced hypnotic state. When you zone out in front of the television, computer monitor or smartphone, you literally become entranced. I remember when my kids were younger, they would be so hypnotized by a television show or video game that I would have to dramatically raise the tone of my voice just to get their attention. If, for example, you have ever been intensely involved into a book that you are reading, and you can mentally visualize the scenes and characters in it, then you have fallen into a low-level trancelike state without even knowing it.

Hypnotic suggestion works by bypassing the critical conscious mind and speaks directly to the unconscious mind in a language that it understands, such as a pattern, association, or metaphor. Theories as to how this is achieved range from hypnotism changing brain activity to saying the person is simply play-acting, in other words, pretending to be a hypnotized person. The most vocal skeptics, however, decry that it is simply a placebo effect, and for instance, if you are sick, you will feel better from just thinking that you will be getting better, that your illness is psychosomatic. They all say basically the same thing though when you get right down to nuts and bolts, that hypnosis works on the unconscious mind.

35

Chapter 3: The Dark Side of Hypnosis

In the 1950s and 60s, the United States CIA (Central Intelligence Agency) was trying to create the perfect killing machine. A program was embarked upon that went by the code name of "Project MKUltra," and "MKUltra" was divided into a plethora of subprograms run by the CIA, FBI, and the U.S military, with names like "Operation Paperclip" and "Project Monarch". This is most definitely not a conspiracy theory. The U.S. government has admitted to it, and many records that have been reclassified show that this horrific program did indeed exist. Not only were American citizens and brave soldiers unknowingly drugged and hypnotized, they were also subjected to inhuman life-threatening situations. One of the biggest scandals' to come out of this project involved hypnotizing and then dosing an American army scientist with LSD. The man's name was Frank Olson, and without his knowledge and consent, the CIA and various other government agencies hypnotized and brainwashed him and gave him massive amounts of the powerful hallucinogenic known as LSD. In the name of science, CIA operatives and doctors lured Frank Olson to a hotel room under false pretenses and spiked his drink with LSD. As you can imagine, Mr. Olson became very agitated and confused by what was happening and ended up busting through a plate glass window on the 23rd floor in complete hysterics and fell to his untimely and tragic death.

The government investigated and found that they had done nothing wrong and called Mr. Olson's death a tragic suicide. The family, of course, knew that it could not be true, so they pushed the government a little harder and it was reluctantly reclassified as a "misadventure".

The surviving family and a good number of other people think that it had really been a murder, especially when records pertaining to the case were reclassified and the illicit drug tests were discovered. Mr. Olson was not the only victim of Project MKUltra, however. There is another story from that project about a man who was repeatedly hypnotized and given LSD to ingest for 145 days straight. Another disturbing document reveals a study where two women were hypnotized using a powerful new technique where one woman was put into a deep hypnotic sleep, and the other woman was told to wake her. If the other woman did not wake up, she was then commanded to pull the trigger of a gun that was given to her, and kill the woman by shooting her in the head. Thankfully, the gun was not loaded, because that is exactly what she did. There was another case of a woman who was hypnotized and told to wait by the phone. Then a call was made to her, and a secret code word was spoken into her ear. At this prompting, the woman then fell into a deep trance state and was compelled to carry a suitcase filled with a fake bomb and place it under a bridge. It's even been said the CIA has used mind control and hypnotism to split a person's personality into different sections where one personality doesn't know what the other is doing in order to enable them to carry out secret covert missions. If they are split into different people with different personalities, it's the perfect setup, just like "The Manchurian Candidate, which was a movie about the government using mind control. A truly evil person or government could use this to plant a person that could get close enough to assassinate a President or even the Pope for that matter. Brainwashing people with hypnotism is nefarious in and of itself, but that depiction is not the first time that hypnotism and mesmerism were misused for evil purposes. Think of a certain man in Germany during the World War II who used his powerful hypnotic technique to inflame a country to war, and convinced the German people that cooking people in big steel ovens was cool.

Hitler did not start out as a great orator. He practiced his body motions in a full-length mirror so he could get them just right. He taught himself to speak with a powerful booming voice that would stimulate the brains of the common

39

folk of Germany. His eyes were so incredible and piercing that even if you were unable to understand the words, you could still feel his powerful animal magnetism that enthralled people. Everything had to be perfect to set the proper tone needed to hypnotize the adoring masses. Hitler would command for giant ceremonies to be held, and hundreds of thousands of men, women, and children waved little flags and soldiers would march in perfect synchronicity while hundreds of runners holding torches would jog through the venue. It was quite a spectacle, and he had them eating out of his hands. Not until it was too late did they snap out of their hypnotic trance and see him for what he really was.

What about today's world? Surely we are not being hypnotized and brainwashed in this modern age? Yes, we are... more than ever. Today's government has so much control over us through the devious use of hypnotic propaganda, that we don't know if we're coming or going. The government tells the major media outlets what to print just to get a reaction that benefits them and furthers their agenda. On any given day you will see the same lead story on the front page of every major newspaper. People are hypnotized by their smart phones, so much so that you can see a video of people falling into open manholes while gazing intently at their video phones. Usually, If they're not immersed in the activity on their phones then they are staring droopy eyed at a computer monitor with their mouths hanging open. Facebook is keeping them hypnotized. The internet is the ultimate hypnotic tool for the government to use in order to enforce its will and keep people nice and calm. We don't want any revolutions, right? The sad part of all of this government control is that we, the citizens, are allowing it to happen. It's not totally fair to blame the citizens for falling prey to the hypnotic trap though; after all, we have been hypnotically programmed since we entered preschool to fall into line. Nowadays, we actually invite a hypnotic device like, Amazon's Alexa machine, into our homes so the government can listen to and record our private conversations.

What needs to be done is that people need to be more aware of the hypnotic control being forced upon them. Educate yourselves and try to be more aware when going about your life. Just give up the mesmerizing screen of the internet for a week. Read alternative papers (as long as it's a good source), be a good citizen, and go out and vote. It's possible to get rid of the people that are trying to control us and replace them with congressmen and senators who will get rid of this "nanny state" that we live in nowadays. Companies hypnotize us every day. They really know how to manipulate our minds by using our senses. We are titillated by sexy images of bikini-clad supermodels and muscular hunks telling us that we can be like them if we just buy the product they are endorsing. It's a form of hypnotism when our leaders tell us the same lies over and over again. It's like Joseph Goebbels said while working as the propaganda minister for Adolph Hitler "If you tell a lie enough times it becomes the truth."

Chapter 4: How Does Hypnotism Work and What Part of the Body and Mind Is Affected?

There are many different theories about how hypnotism affects the human mind, and making sense of them can be a bit confusing to the layman or person not familiar with hypnotism and its terminology.

The art of hypnosis is thought to function by altering our state of consciousness in a particular way that the left-hand side of the brain is switched completely off, while the right-hand side is made to be a lot more alert. The techniques cause us to reach deeper into the subconscious mind.

Some people believe that hypnotism is nothing but a placebo effect that works on the mind of a person with a low mentality and constitution. A person who is a hypochondriac and wasn't really sick in the first place. That is the skeptic's take on the whole business of hypnotism.

Another popular theory is that the act of hypnotism totally changes your brain when under the hypnotic spell of a practitioner of hypnosis. They talk about everything from overcoming a change from the actual chemistry of the brain to the physical makeup of the structure of the brain, if they are to be believed.

Ernest Hilgard said that hypnosis splits consciousness into two different parts known as the follower and the hidden observer.

The hidden observer theory states that a person who is undergoing hypnosis becomes an observer to the act of being hypnotized. He taught that a person undergoing a hypnotic change of state can observe pain without actually feeling the pain. Hilgard thought that we all have two separate beings sharing our life, beings he called "the hidden observer" and "the follower."

The social cognitive view of hypnosis tells us that hypnosis is a mostly learned behavior. People who follow this line of thinking believe that hypnosis can be achieved only in people who know how those who are hypnotized are supposed to behave.

Be sure to remember that these are just two theories, and nobody really understands how hypnotism **truly** works on the human psyche.

Kirsch's response expectancy theory is based on the idea that "what people experience depends partly on what they expect to experience." The expectation is that if you go into a hypnotherapy session with the idea in your head that you will be cured you most probably will achieve that outcome. Likewise, if you go into your session with a negative attitude and believe it to be a worthless science, or if you're just too stubborn to accept help, you will most certainly **not** be affected or helped by a hypnotic session with a qualified hypnotherapy practitioner.

The dissociated control theory of hypnosis was conceived by two psychological researchers by the names of Woody and Bowers as another attempt to explain hypnotic theory. The conscious and subconscious were expressed in terms of <u>executive control</u> and the <u>lower control subsystems</u>.

What their theory was trying to explain was that hypnotism goes something like this... When the subject is undergoing the hypnotic trance state, they will experience a process of separation of the executive control sections and the lower control sections of the sub-conscious intellect.

A fantastic example of this theory is the act of driving and interacting with traffic norms and attention paid to the act of driving your car.

When you first get your license to drive you are in the "conscious competence" state. That is, you know how to drive a car. However, you still need to remain alert, and every process and action you make behind the wheel of the vehicle is consciously thought out and acted upon.

Wherein after driving for many months and you are a whole lot more comfortable with driving a car and following the rules of the road, you enter a hypnotic state known as "unconscious competency". This is the state that you will usually be driving in for the rest of your life. People in this state find themselves able to think about two tasks simultaneously. They are, to a certain extent, shifting and switching gears, checking their mirrors and watching the road at an unconscious level, while simultaneously thinking about a date with their sweetie pie on Friday. In this example, they are participating in two separate experiences but are only aware of one. They have dissociated the conscious from the subconscious.

The last theory of hypnotic control over the mind is the "cold control" theory. This theory was developed in 2007, and a lot of practitioners use this method. It's the newest hypnotic theory being used today.

As far as the different parts of the brain affected by hypnotism, well, get ready for some big words. The hypnotic state is for the most part associated with the activation of several key locations in the subject's brain. Mainly left-sided cortical areas involving occipital, parietal, precentral, premotor, and ventrolateral prefrontal cortices are activated. Men and women that are easily and quickly hypnotized also show much higher activity on the left side of the prefrontal cortex.

Some right-sided activated areas of the human brain are the occipital and anterior cingulate cortices. The anterior cingulate gyrus area is also activated, and in a hypnotized individual, reduced activity is noticed in the dorsal anterior cingulate.

Parts of the body that can be affected are the legs, arms, back and even the ears. Every part of the body has been reputed to have been healed by the powers of the hypnotic trance. Another concept the average person doesn't realize, is that for someone who wants to improve their personal performance and overcome fear and crippling anxiety, hypnotism doesn't just affect your body physically, it can mentally allow you to *create* certain situations and outcomes. It's a form of self-hypnosis known as creative visualization and some very famous performers and athletes swear by it. The important thing to remember is that your brain **does not** know the difference between what has actually happened and what you imagine happening. In other words, the brain doesn't know the difference between a creative visualized image and the real thing. A lot of performers mentally prepare themselves for a concert or a performance by imagining themselves singing their hearts out to loud rounds of clapping from the audience, or an actor or actress will get themselves into a positive hypnotic mental state and really get into the character that they are emulating.

The late actor Heath Ledger locked himself in a hotel room alone for months to prepare for his role as the Joker in a Batman movie. He wanted to hypnotize himself to the point that he **was** the Joker. Olympic athletes, football stars, runners and a whole host of other sports stars also use it. A runner, for example, relaxes and gets his or her mind clear and then simply imagines themselves running and winning the race, again and again. In their brains, they have run that course a hundred times. That's not saying that you don't need actual practice, because if you want to play sports at a high level, you should also actively pursue behaviors to improve your physical body. It's like Connor McGregor (an Irish UFC fighter) says, "when preparation meets opportunity, it's a beautiful thing".

Chapter 5: Hypnotic Interview and the Pre-Talk

Hypnosis induces a person to go into an extreme hypnotic state, and anyone can be hypnotized if they don't resist the hypnotic efforts of a hypnotist. In hypnosis therapy, only a light to medium hypnotic trance is usually needed. In some cases though, a deeper hypnotic trance state is necessary to achieve mutual goals of physical and mental wellness.

The most important thing that is done by or with a hypnotist before their session is to put the patient at ease, and there are various ways to do this. The subject should feel a sense of being safe and protected. You can't get a person into a proper frame of mind to be induced into the hypnotic trance state if they are ill at ease. Remember this might be their first experience with seeing a hypnotic practitioner or being put into a hypnotic state, and they will never be suggestable to the hypnotic process if they **do not** feel at ease and relaxed in your care.

This goes for the area that you use to practice your hypnotic skills in too. The room should be closed off to outer stimuli since you cannot have a million little distractions disturbing the hypnotic experience for the subject. Have your office/work area as comfortable and pleasing to the eye as you are able to make it. Keep the parking lot of your office maintained well. A pleasant environment is key to creating a relaxing atmosphere. So always keep this in mind if and when you decide to pursue hypnosis as a healing or entertainment vocation.

You can never know if someone that you are attempting to hypnotize has had a poor experience with another hypnotic health provider. You need to ask about this during the hypnosis sessions interview because it could be a factor in helping a person become relaxed and fall into a safe and helpful hypnotic trance state.

During your interview, try to find out if this person seeking your help has been led to believe that hypnotism is some type of magic by their religion. Believe it or not, some religions may still be under the wrong assumption that hypnotic endeavors are somehow related to the occult world. Assure the interviewee that hypnosis is not involved in the dark arts. Put this person at ease and reassure them that there is nothing sacrilegious about it.

During the interview make sure to educate your hypnotic subject about the hypnotic process. Let them know how the hypnotic trance state will help them to grow and become better people, better citizens, better husbands or wives, and maybe even better lovers. Educate them on how a great many physical and mental problems can be cured (or at least put in check) to a certain extent by a hypnotic session and a laying on of hands if that's your particular notch in the hypnotism business broomstick. It's not just that though. A person could be made to give up smoking or to lose weight, hypnotically, if given the chance. It's done all of the time, everywhere across the United States in hotel lobbies, meeting rooms, school gyms, and water buffalo lodge meetings. Just the other day, I heard an advertisement over FM radio, persuading overweight people or heavy smokers to come to a seminar at the local Holiday Inn to be hypnotized to lose those unwanted pounds or stop the disgusting, money wasting habit of cigarette abuse. I've never personally seen a weight loss or stop smoking hypnotic session; however, I assume that they must work because they are still being attended by a great number of people.

You can use the interview before the hypnotic session to learn if the subject has any serious medical issue(s) you should be aware of before performing hypnotism. Always make sure they don't have serious heart conditions, high blood pressure, etc., since you don't want to aggravate a preexisting condition in your subject that might cause harm to them. Also, if the person asking to be treated with hypnosis has a problem with chronic pain, make sure that you have them get a physical exam by a certified medical doctor to manage the affliction before beginning any hypnosis sessions.

During the pre-hypnosis interview, verify the identity of your subject. It's during the pre-hypnosis interview that you would make sure that you have got the right contact information for them, including next of kin. It's extremely unlikely that something will happen, but they might collapse with a heart attack when they walk in your front door. By all means call for immediate medical assistance before you call the family. However, you do want to let a family member or close friend know that the subject is getting medical attention and may need their assistance. The subject will obviously be more comfortable at the hospital with someone that they know and that knows their medical history more extensively.

Checking into phobias or things the subject does not like – such as depth, height, insects, darkness, etc. – is vital. Knowing these things will help you avoid using them during any visualization you want to use with your subject. You definitely don't want to scare your subject, or bring up a person or event that causes them duress. You do want them to be as relaxed as possible, and that way the subject will more easily fall into the hypnotic trance state.

It's a fantastic idea to build a rapport with the person that you are planning on hypnotizing. That's really just one more reason that it is very important to conduct a pre-interview with your hypnotic subject before actually inducing them into a deep trance state. The more they feel they know you and begin to trust you completely, the easier it will be to help them with whatever their situation happens to be.

After gathering all of this information from your subject or client, it's time to start talking your subject into the hypnotic trance state. Start by having your subject shut off their smartphone and also don't forget to shut off your own phones. There should be absolutely **no interruptions** during the session. Lock the door, draw the shades and curtains, and put on some relaxing instrumental music. Have the hypnotic subject sit comfortably or recline on a comfortable couch. Being relaxed is important to what you want to accomplish with your client or subject. You may want to burn some herbs or incense to set the mood or even some essential oils that are conducive to relaxation, such as lavender.

Doing these things will get your client or subject relaxed and ready to be hypnotized, and you will be able to start the process of putting them under a hypnotic trance suggestion in relative peace and comfort, and with an atmosphere of safety and respect for both participants.

Chapter 6: Trancework

Everyone's experience of hypnosis is as unique as the person who practices hypnotism or the person becomes the subject of hypnotic suggestion. It really is limitless. There are some people who can experience very deep states of hypnosis, while for others, only a light state is possible.

There are 4 trance states, and they are as follows: Light trance, apparent somnambulism, true somnambulism, and coma, (or Esdaile), state.

THE LIGHT TRANCE:

Almost everybody is able to achieve this level of hypnosis, called light trance hypnosis. All it really is, is a deep relaxation state and solid focused state of being. A lot of therapists claim that it is a worthless state in which nothing important can be accomplished. Still, there are a great deal of people who can go no deeper than this, who will still be able to achieve amazing results from a light trance. The hypnotic suggestion, especially at this depth will allow you to achieve a great deal and could be of great therapeutic benefit to you. It is not the hypnosis that will achieve results for you, but the therapy that is provided within the hypnotic state will help you achieve your desired results.

At the hypnotic level known as the "light trance," you will still be very aware of what is going on around you. You will still be able to hear distracting voices and noises in adjoining rooms so you will have to concentrate on ignoring these things.

You may think that not much can be achieved at this level. However, this is not true. A person could have a lot of helpful suggestions embedded at this lowest level of the four hypnotic trances.

APPARENT SOMNAMBULISM:

Apparent somnambulism is a state of blissful relaxation and well-being, and a mesmerizing state where you are very open to suggestions from outside sources. But, not so deep into the hypnotic trance that you wouldn't feel the prick from a needle being jammed in your eye. Apparent somnambulism is just what it sounds like... apparent, as in, not somnambulism. It's a state of hypnotic suggestion that is just a bit deeper than a light hypnotic trance but, not as deep as what is known as true somnambulism.

TRUE SOMNAMBULISM:

What is this thing that we call true somnambulism? Let's see if we can figure it out. The truly somnambulistic state, in which the mind, as well as the body, is totally relaxed, is considered by some therapists to be an absolute necessity for hypnotic suggestion to have any useful effect. The theory is that it is conducive to a state of barren "nothingness". The mind is totally relaxed and doing nothing, not even thinking that it is blank. It is in the ultimately suggestible state; since there are no thoughts going on, the conscious critical faculty, (which is the internal barometer we use to judge right and wrong) simply isn't able to overcome or override outside suggestions.

Another name for true somnambulism is "sleepwalking. Sleepwalking is the phenomenon of combined sleep and wakefulness. Sleepwalking affects 3.6% of U.S. citizens.

COMA STATE OR ESDAILE STATE:

A coma is a state of unconsciousness that a person cannot be awakened from. A person cannot respond to pain, light, speech or other stimuli while in a coma. A coma **is not** a state of hypnotic trance, and a hypnotist cannot induce a person to fall into a coma state through the power of hypnotism.

HYPNOTIC INDUCTION TECHNIQUES

Relaxation technique

Therapists usually ask you to make yourself feel at home and be comfy during an introduction meeting. They may even provide you with a soft couch to lay on. Why? Are they just being courteous? The truth is, it's more than that. Therapists use relaxation as a common method to induce hypnosis. If you are relaxed, you are likely to fall in a trance quicker, and your mind becomes more open to accept suggestions.

Listed are some of the usual methods to promote relaxation:

- Be comfortable.
- Lay down.
- In your head, start to count down.
- Control your breathing.
- Tense your muscles and then relax.
- Speak in a calm, soft tone.

Handshake technique

The father of hypnotherapy, Milton Erickson, became famous for using a handshake technique to get a person into a hypnotic trance. Handshake is a common greeting, but in hypnosis, it can be more than just a gesture. Hypnotists do not just shake hands in a normal way, they interrupt the mind of the subject by grabbing his wrist or pulling him forward to break the balance. Because the pattern established by the mind of the subject was interrupted, the client's subconscious mind will suddenly be open to suggestions.

Eyes Cues Technique

The brain has two spheres – the conscious and creative side (right) and the practical and subconscious side (left). Basically, when we are in a conversation with someone, we look for feedback just to know how they feel or react to what we say. Watch your subject's eyes. Are they looking to the right? Or are they looking to the left? Remember, when they're looking to the right, that suggests that they are conscious of the current situation, and if they are looking to the left, that means they are in subconscious thought.

Visualization Technique

You can use visualization to induce your subject into a hypnotic trance and make suggestions. For instance, ask your subject to visualize a room that they know very well. Instruct them to visualize each detail in that room: the windows, the smell, the lighting, the color of the wall, the texture of the floor. Then, ask them to visualize a room they do not know, such as your office. As they struggle to remember the exact details of the room they are less familiar with, they open their minds to suggestions.

Arm Levitation Technique

You can perform this by asking your subject to close their eyes. Then, ask them to notice the difference between their arms. They might say their arms are heavy or light. Subconsciously, they will enter a trance and lift their arms or make their mind believe they have lifted their arms. Either way, the induction is a success.

Sudden Shock/Falling Backwards Technique

As with the handshake technique, a subject in shock can enter into a trance. You might have heard about "trust falls". The feeling of falling backward can put the body into shock. Thus, it opens the mind to accept suggestions. Of course, you must catch your subject and be very careful not to drop him/her.

Hypnotic Trigger Technique

There are several forms of hypnotic triggers. A trigger lets the subconscious remember a desired feeling or action that is suggested while under hypnosis. Here are some examples:

- Finger snap

- Clap

- Sound of ball

- Opening eyes

- Standing or sitting

Touch Technique

In this technique, the hypnotist or psychiatrist will put the subject into a relaxed state of mind. Then, gently, the hypnotist will tap the subject's hands with his/her own with a slight pressure. Next, with a pen held directly in front of the subject, they will follow it with their eyes while visualizing a perfect place in their mind. This technique needs to be repeated several times during each session. Every after session I have with this technique, I am always relaxed and feel a lot better.

Chapter 7: Trance Deepeners

A trance deepener is something that allows the hypnotist to take the subject deeper into a hypnotic trance state. Sometimes they're necessary, sometimes they're not. But basically a trance deepener is something that a hypnotist uses after they put someone into a trance. They give them suggestions like, "...finding yourself going deeper and deeper...," "...finding yourself feeling more and more relaxed...," "...the more relaxed you feel, the deeper you will go into your trance...," "...you feel as if you're going down..."

<u>Staircase Deepener</u>

Tell your subject to imagine a beautiful staircase, wooden or carpeted, (their choice) with a beautiful wooden railing. Now, have them intensely visualize that the staircase has 10 steps leading down. As they go farther down the steps, their trance becomes deeper and deeper until they reach the last stair and step off, and become deeply hypnotized and entranced.

Awareness Deepener

The hypnotic practitioner will invite his/her subject to relax and remain calm. The subject will be directed to think about his/her total body, to think about their feet and then be aware of them. Direct them to focus their thoughts on their feet, then move to their knees and be aware of them becoming more relaxed. They just need to be aware of each body part named, and then imagine that body part completely relaxing. Next, move on to their heart beat. The subject needs to be aware of the beating of their heart and then consciously slow it and calm it down. By the time you finish, your subject will be brought into a relaxing trance state.

Candle Deepener

"Imagine in your mind's eye a single lit candle. You can imagine a candle color that you enjoy and will relax you. The color really does not matter. Focus your mind on the flame of the candle, and see the colors within the flame. Notice the movement and dancing of the flame, as the yellows and reds swirl around. You may notice other colors in the flame, orange, blue, white, or maybe some other color. As you see colors within the flame, you will begin to relax more and more, going deeper and deeper, as you enjoy the sensation of relaxation and hypnotic feelings. And as the flame flickers, try to focus - and if you find your mind wandering away from the flame of the candle, just bring it gently back again through concentration. Focus now, on the wax body of that candle in your mind's eye. As you see the first trickle of melting wax, your mind and psyche will be in a totally relaxed hypnotic trance. Now imagine that you are actually that candle, a candle of total relaxation. Warm and soothing, melting away any stress or tension, as you begin to sink into a deeper trance. Picture the chair that you are sitting in, as a candleholder, and that your muscles, like the wax of your candle of relaxation, are melting into the chair and that you are becoming yourself, a candle of relaxation.

Telephone Deepener

A session where the subject is not in the room is the telephone deepener. It's not the ideal thing for helping a person by using your hypnotic suggestion, but it is an option. A session might go a little something like this: "Now I want you to visualize yourself lying on a comfortable raft gently floating on the water, and just imagine the sun shining down on your face." "Feel the warmth of the sun on your face, the coolness of the water on your skin as it washes gently against the side of the raft ever so gently." "Just allowing yourself to feel the soft, gentle rocking as I count you down even one more time with 5-4-3-2-1- 0 even deeper sleep, deeper relaxation". If you can't get to a hypnotherapist, or a hypnotherapist can't get to where you are, the next best thing is to conduct a telephone trace deepener or hypnotic session.

Mirroring Deepener

If you are watching a basketball game and you're totally engrossed in it, you may find yourself mirroring a player who is about to shoot a ball to the ring. You'll realize your arms move involuntarily as if you are going to shoot a ball. Hypnotists can help create these hypnotic functions that will control your muscles to induce you into a very powerful hypnotic state.

Stealth Deepener

Surely, there's an occasion in our life where we are in a boring situation, for instance, a seminar or dull lecture. We get totally bored find ourselves in a deep daydream. Bored people are usually very easy to get into the trance.

Pace and Lead Deepener

If you tell your clients that they will get tired quickly, then they will get tired very quickly. Your client will highly likely be into the trance quickly because they believe they need to obey the hypnotist's command. This happens because the client makes himself believe he needs to follow what the hypnotist demands.

Eye Fixation Deepener

In this method, the hypnotist will ask the client to gaze at an item or keep a specific place in mind. This is done by letting the client relax and look up in order to clear their mind. This technique completely relies on the eyes; letting the eyes become tired to get the subject into an intense trance state.

Rapid Induction Deepener

This technique (mostly) relies on distracting the client by pulling them sideways or forward, then commanding them to sleep. Not all subjects respond to this hypnosis though, but if it works, it works instantly. This phenomenon is called *Tonic Immobility*. Tonic immobility is a natural state of paralysis which animals enter, often referred to as animal hypnosis. Its function though is not yet known to health professionals. Please do not use this technique on a subject with heart conditions or any type of anxiety.

Pendulum Deepener

The hypnotic practitioner can use a pendulum to help deepen a hypnotic subject's trance state. A pendulum can be something as simple as a common bolt and nut on a string. Have the subject follow the swinging pendulum back and forth, as you hold it in front of them. Just have them simply relax and follow the directions you give them, and soon they will soon be in a deep hypnotic state.

Detailed Breathing Deepener

In detailed breathing, the focus is on the strength of the subject's awareness to perceive the smallest detail. When breathing, they need to focus on the sensations of a specific part of their nose, such as the tip or right nostril. Make the target of his/her attention as specific as possible by focusing on the smallest details. They can focus on an earlobe or a fingertip, it doesn't matter what it is. If this is difficult to do, focus on larger areas of the body such as the expansion of the ribs.

Chapter 8: What Signs to Look for When Gauging the Depth of a Trance

Temperature

One thing to look for in a person in a deep hypnotic trance is a very noticeable rise in a person's body and oral temperature. So keep your studio or office, or the room you are practicing in at a comfortable level. You want your practice area to be as comfortable as it can be to encourage a pleasant and productive hypnotic session.

Head Dropping

Head dropping is a great indicator that a person is in a hypnotic trance. The head should be hanging naturally and not in an alarming way. As has been said in previous chapters, the hypnotic patient must be totally relaxed to get the full benefit from the hypnotic trance state and trance induction.

Shoulders Slumped

If the hypnotic subject has a slump to their shoulders, it's a pretty good sign that the subject is in a relaxed hypnotic state. It's a big giveaway, since you don't see too many people that are tense with sloping relaxed shoulders.

Breathing Changes

A person under the hypnosis of a hypnotic practitioner will experience a very relaxed pattern of breathing. Slow and methodical and somewhat shallow, but not too shallow, of course, that the subject stops breathing. Make sure to always keep an eye on their breathing.

Skin Tone

During a hypnotic session, a subject's skin may droop a little bit and hang a little looser off of the body, and it may also become a little softer. It's a very strange change indeed.

Skin Complexion

Shockingly, the color of your skin may even change a little bit in a hypnotic state. Your skin might actually take on a lighter color for the duration of the hypnotic session. However, not to worry, it will turn back to a normal tone when you are finished.

Facial and Body Movements

You may notice slight facial movements during the hypnotic trance session, but don't be concerned, it's natural. As a matter of fact, your face is twitching and moving a lot when you are at rest. It's mostly involuntary muscle reaction. Once again, it is likely that the heart and pulse rate will slow down. As a matter of record, it **should** happen during the hypnotic trance session because of the relaxed state of the subject. Your subject will most likely lick their lips, however, it should slow down or stop once the subject falls deeper into the hypnotic trance state. You will notice the patient but it swallowing too, but it will slow down once the hypnotic session starts and the subject becomes more deeply entranced.

Eyes

Rapid eye movements may occur as a hypnotic subject is undergoing a normal treatment, so don't be alarmed by it. It's just REM (rapid eye movements), and it happens every time you go to sleep, it's just a very relaxed state. You should expect to see less blinking in a hypnotized person, and you might notice a little tearing. Tearing that is not associated with a painful memory that has been induced, but tearing from natural tearing to keep your eyes from drying out. The eyes may be glazed on the hypnotic patient, that's okay and expected in a person undergoing a hypnotic trance. As a matter of fact, if the eyes aren't glazed over, the subject may not yet be in a deep hypnotic state. Another thing that might happen is for the subject to be transfixed in their gaze.

How can you tell if someone is faking being hypnotized?-

If you think someone is lying to you, listen to the person's voice. Listen for words or phrases that are used often, and to the words they say in a low or monotone voice. If they're lying, they will usually change their tone to high. That shows that they're uncomfortable. If your subject is hiding something, they will usually say very little to avoid getting caught in a story they can't justify or that just doesn't make any sense. They will also avoid using the words "I," "my," or "me" to make their statements less dishonest. They also tend to avoid discussing how they feel, and would rather tell stories in a general way. They may also touch their nose or neck because they can't look you in the eyes. These subtle cues are known as *shielding*. Their subconscious mind tries to shield itself from lies by covering up the mouth, eyes, or other weak areas like their belly or throat.

Chapter 9: How to Hypnotize Anyone, Anywhere, Anytime

Anyone, anywhere, anytime can be hypnotized. It's been said that a person needs to want to be hypnotized for hypnotism to be effective. I don't believe that, because I've heard and read stories of people being hypnotized against their will (especially if you're talking about the government). They have invented ways of bringing a person under their nefarious control. However, the techniques in this book are for fun, entertainment, and therapeutic use only.

One of the easiest ways to hypnotize someone is with the "progressive relaxation" technique.

> Have the subject you're working with sit or lie down in a comfortable position.

Talk slowly in a soothing voice. Just tell the subject to "Take a deep breath and as you let it out, close your eyes and begin to feel yourself relaxing.

Have your subject focus their attention on different parts of their body and relax them, systematically. You can use words such as "Now become aware of your arms and now relax your arms, just let them grow more and more comfortable, let the muscles become loose and limp and even more relaxed." Make sure that you repeat this for every part of the body, as the subject needs to relax completely.

Sprinkle your language with plenty of positive reinforcements.
Repeat if necessary until the subject is completely relaxed. Depending on the person, you may have to repeat the whole procedure a few times. When you're ready to bring them back to

awareness, say "I'm going to count to five, when I reach five or before, your eyes will open, and you'll feel relaxed and refreshed". Count to five slowly with your voice getting a little less soothing and a little more "awake" with each number. When you reach four and their eyes aren't open, you'll need to say "On the next number your eyes will open, and you'll feel relaxed and refreshed. Keep your eyes open, feeling relaxed and refreshed."

How to hypnotize someone for fun:

1. **Educate yourself about hypnotism (Which is the purpose of this wonderful educational book!).** Become familiar with the techniques you will be using. You need to practice often. After all, you want it to work so you don't look silly in front of anyone.

2. Recruit a volunteer to help you out. Get more than one volunteer, because sometimes the hypnotic procedure doesn't take on a hypnotic subject. This is always a lot of fun at a social gatherings. Find yourself a handsome fellow or attractive woman and ask them to participate in the fun. You may also get yourself a date.

3. Safety is job one as they say. Think about the safety of all participants. Having fun is the main goal, but remember, safety is a MUST. Have the subject sit or lie down on a sturdy surface area, even the floor is good, for the purpose of your session.

3. Begin by speaking directly to your subject. Temper your voice and use your words carefully. Your words are one of the most powerful tools you have when practicing hypnosis. The main thing is to repeatedly say things that suggest how people should feel or behave in a certain way. Eventually, they should start responding to the words you are repeating. Hypnosis is a process in which you may not see instantaneous results. It may take a couple of minutes.

4. **Maintain eye contact with your subject to strengthen your bond with them during the session.** Observe your subject and look for visual clues that they are going into a hypnotic trance. Having good eye contact is extremely important when you are attempting to hypnotize someone. This is true whether or not you are practicing covert or general hypnosis. Focus on one subject at a time, and make sure that you are maintaining steady, consistent eye contact.

5. **Make the session fun with your subject by all means.** You can tell when someone is responding to your hypnotic suggestions. Put on some popular music and convince the subject that they are alone in their room, so it's okay to dance. Make them believe that they are in a dance contest or even on a popular dance show. Suggest that the subject is an animal and have them get down on all fours and bark like a dog or slither across the floor like a duck-billed platypus. GREAT FUN!

Hypnotizing a dog:

Step 1: Be in a calm, quiet place,

If you want the trust, compliance, and attention of your dog, then you need to give them a comfortable, calm, relaxing environment. Find a place they are less likely to be distracted or agitated, that is free from noises, other animals, or other people,

Step 2: Use a gentle and soft touch.

To build trust and connection, hypnotists use touch on the arms, shoulders, or other vulnerable spots. This is also applicable to pets. Give your pet a gentle touch by either stroking their belly, back, or head. This will put them at ease.

Step 3: Provide relaxing sounds

Repeating soothing phrases can help your dog stay calm. Make sure your pet is comfortable. They will usually get comfortable just by hearing your voice. Calming music is also helpful.

Step 4: Holding Position

After following the first three steps, your dog may appear to be almost in a trancelike state. To get your pet into a deeper trance, shift your dog into a submissive position. Some folks recommend lulling your dog, by placing them on your lap with their rump close to you and their head placed between your knees. Others suggest shifting your pet onto their back and holding them under your arms. Then, stroke their belly until their limbs become limp.

Step 5: Tonic State

You'll know you have hypnotized your dog by their body language. They need to be in a tonic state (see Chapter 7 for more information). Your dog will be completely still and limp. At this point, you should be able to release them, and they will still be in a tonic state. See if they respond when you poke their limbs. To wake them up from the tonic state, you must do it by a clap or a call.

Conclusion

Thank you for reading *Hypnosis: How to Hypnotize Anyone (The Beginner's Guide to Hypnotism)*. We hope it was informative and provided you with effective tools you need to achieve your goals with hypnosis.

The next step is to go out and have some fun with it, or explore hypnotism as an interesting new career choice. Go out into the world with a fantastic new skill! The possibilities are really limitless. The only limit, as they say, is your desire, dreams and the intuitive drive to better yourself and the world around you and try new exciting new things. This skill could even take you to different parts of the world. Imagine visiting a faraway beach hotel in an exotic location to give a presentation and also have a chance to practice your hypnotic trade.

You will be a huge hit at any party or gathering of friends and family once you learn the art of hypnotism. It's a lot of fun and good times. With the fantastic knowledge in this book and maybe even further research on your own, you can be blowing minds at your next work gathering. If you decide to pursue a career in hypnotism, you could be doing this in front of large crowds of people. You could even become a hypnotist that helps people lose weight or stop smoking, and from what I know about the subject, it pays pretty well.

NLP 2.0

NLP 2.0:

The Ultimate Guide to
Neuro Linguistic Programming

How to Rewire Your Brain and Create the Life You
Want and Become the Person You Were Meant to Be

Kyle Faber

CAC Publishing LLC
ISBN: 978-1-948489-20-1 (paperback)
ISBN: 978-1-948489-20-1 (ebook)
Kyle Faber

This book is dedicated to those that wish to shatter through the glass ceiling you have inadvertently put over your head. To those that want to break free from the confinements they have subconsciously locked themselves in. You can achieve things you never thought possible by learning to rewire your brain. This book is dedicated to those that wish to learn the inner confines of their brain and catapult themselves to successes they once thought impossible.

Preface

At 3, our minds are such that we absorb all that is placed in our field of observation – a field that can be pretty wide. Objects and concepts placed within that field get imprinted in our mind with a quality that is almost photographic.

There are some who think that the mind is empty, making it easier to absorb, at that age, but that's not even close to the truth. Three-year-olds are able to absorb almost perfectly, not because there is nothing in there, but because their interest keeps them focused. As a 30-year old, or even a 60-year old, if you could muster the same sort of distraction-free focus, then you will be able to absorb at the same rate – theoretically.

In practice, it's not just being distraction-free that makes the difference; it's also about how we are altered by our experiences and how we are all different from one moment to the next. Heraclitus said that a man never steps into the same river twice, because the river has changed, and so has the man.

When I was 3, the lot of us piled into a station-wagon, bound for a picnic at a farm three towns over. I loved road trips, even as a toddler. On this particular road trip, we were surrounded by farms for miles in every direction. The only thing that changed was what the fences were guarding. Most farms had crops, and some were livestock – herds of cows, fields of horses, and mobs of sheep. We came upon a stretch of farms that, together, must have had, what seemed, like a million heads. It was my first experience, so my father stopped the car so we could take in the sight and sounds of this herd. My uncle carried me and we stood by the curb watching this giant herd. I asked him what they were and he said, "Sheep", out of earshot from where my father was. They were cows.

We drove along for a few more minutes, and this time we came across another farm which was unique to all the other farms in the area. It was like a field of snow since all the sheep were still in full coat. This time when I asked my uncle, he told me they were cows. They were, of course, sheep. He must have thought it was funny. I didn't know any better. But it stuck. In my three-year old brain, cows were sheep and sheep were cows. My father found out this comedy of 'errors' later that day when he and I had a debate over cows and sheep and he couldn't understand why I kept pointing to cows and proudly calling out sheep. I didn't like it one bit when he kept saying I was wrong. I am up in years now but catch me on an off day, and I would need a moment's pause to mentally re-confirm cows from sheep. Moral of the story: be careful what you tell a 3-year old, it sticks fast.

Neuro-Linguistic Programming (NLP) is just a high-flying, technical-sounding name for how we associate things based on sensory input –

especially sound, and specifically, the sounds we make when we utter words.

To be more specific, NLP is how we associate things and events based on a pair, or more, of sensory inputs and cogitations.

Let me unpack that.

We attach words to meanings, objects, and concepts; and conversely, attach concepts, objects, and phenomena to words. When we do this, our conscious mind has a frame of reference to attach to things. Think about a file cabinet. Open it and you find lots of files. Inside each file, you have the full specifications of one object. Let's say that object is a car. Inside the file, you have every possible description of that car and images. Now imagine if there is no name on that file, how would you be able to know where all that information is located? Conversely, as soon as you place a sticker on that file that reads, "My Car" instantly, you now have an object that you can define, and the one word object that summarizes that object is the term "My Car".

When my crazy uncle pointed to a cow and said sheep, I promptly took a mental picture of the cow, placed it in a folder in my mind's filing cabinet, and labeled it "Sheep". We call that association and our conscious mind is all about associations.

Every label we attach is attached to things we associate with sounds. I took the mental image of a four-legged beast that had short horns, a tail, and so on; I put it in a file and labeled it with a sound. That sound sounded like "shhh" "eeee" "puh".

In the time before language, early humans used sounds most close to the object or the situation of the object. So it's reasonable to assume that they could have called cows "mooo" and sheep "baaaah". Can you picture how that would have come about when the first caveman was trying to describe the cow he just saw grazing, to his neighbor?

Association. It's the sound we give the file that contains the information of the object. So, the object is the thing that is being observed. The fruit of that observation (the data, the specifications, the descriptions) is then placed in that file, and associated with the sound – the file's name. That's why sometimes you can say one word, and trigger a thought of something else that you associate it with. For instance, when I hear the word "Titanic", I associate it with tragedy, iceberg, drowning and so on.

The person doing that observation, by the way, is called the subject. So to put it all together, we can think of the process as this:

The information of an object, derived from observation by the subject, is placed in a file and that file is associated with a sound. At 3, I associated the sound of "shhhhhheeeeeeepuh" with a cow.

In essence, that's what NLP is all about.

In his quest for a quick laugh, my uncle programmed my neurons with the language that depicted cows as sheep, and it stayed that way for a long time.

Introduction

Life is as simple as we make it to be because we have the power to choose how we interpret all things that we experience. That is an amazing power and is afforded to all of us. What we believe, how we associate different things and how we give meaning to them creates our set of stimuli.

Take for example western and eastern post meal niceties. In some cultures, burping after a meal is considered polite; in fact, it is considered rude if you don't. While in some cultures, it is downright disgusting and rude. So which culture is right?
The sound of the burp is associated with all that is good in one culture while it is associated with all that is bad in the other culture. The burp itself is just a bodily function; it is innocuous, neither good nor bad.

It is what we make it. That is power, isn't it? Before we get started with the next chapter, I am going to show you a couple of exercises that are rather funny but highly effective in being able to change how you react to things.

When I was in college, I took a Public Speaking class my freshman year. It's one of the most memorable classes in all my college years. I had a larger than life instructor who was able to drive home the most subtle of points and deflate the most uncomfortable situations by altering his perception of the situation.

When graduation came around I actually had to give a speech in front of the whole graduating class, it was tough imagining the crowd. The audience was no longer just classmates, as it had been in speech class, now it was the entire school and dignitaries from government and business leaders, one of whom was to be my boss's boss at my new job that fall. To say I was in panic would be, to put it mildly.

I consulted with my former speech instructor and he gave me the simplest advice. He told me to go stand out there and imagine all those people sitting on the toilet. I have a vivid imagination. So when I imagined it that way on graduation morning, instead of turning cold and quivering, I was holding myself back from busting a gut laughing. I delivered the speech in fine style and used that trick many times after that. I've let go of that crutch now since I just see people as they are and not anything that I need to fear, but it was great advice and that one thing he thought me five minutes before graduation was the most useful lesson of all my life up to that point.

We can choose to make this existence a complicated set of mistake and perception-driven consequences, or we can adjust our life by taking control of the most important aspect of everything that comes across our path. How we take it is more important than what it is. Don't reinvent the wheel by trying to search for the higher truth in everything, just take it the way you need to so that you get the best out of it.

If you are in an interview with a Wall Street maverick, you can either be afraid of him or imagine he is a mouse. How you see him determines how you behave, and just by doing that you turn the tables. He would respect you more if you were able to be bold than if you cowered in fear. Right?

That's how you use NLP and that is the first exercise we will put in place at the end of this chapter.

Words and Sounds

We are driven by sounds, aren't we? When you hear the lyrics of your favorite song, what drives you more, the melody, or the lyrics? Both, I think; because lyrics are sounds too, except they are more organized and they pull up different files in your filing system. When you listen to the thunder of a talented motivational speaker; or when you empathize with the words of a plea for help, words are at the heart of these messages. Words are the carriers of an emotional response to these situations, and that gives us insight into the link between words, mind, body, soul, and accomplishment.

How so?

We assign complex notions under the explicit and implicit definition of words. Here is an example. Think of the word "daddy" or "papa". It ordinarily means a paternal parent - father. On its own, it is a noun with a specific meaning, but to you, that means something special, as it does to me. But both our attachments to the word are totally different because over the years that word has been given a meaning by the man that comes to now represent that word.

If you were to compare mindsets to a computer program, it would be a rather striking similarity in many of the components that make up the two. The first is that most programs are designed to interact and do so by looking for input. Contrast that to the way a human being interacts with his or her environment - also an interactive dance between the person and the environment. Imagine, it's a warm day. When it gets to a certain point, the person feels warm - which is an input, and when a certain level is reached, that input triggers a response - for instance, the determination is that it is warm and that something needs to be done about it. So the impulse to get up and flip on the fan is triggered. If it gets past a certain level, then there is another trigger that creates the impulse to turn on the air conditioning or have a cold shower.

The point is that there are three components in a computer action and there are three components in a human action: Input, processing, and output. These components are bound together by the program, which is most notably located in the processing part of the sequence. There are numerous programs that do numerous things and these programs can be nested or combined in any number of ways to create complex actions.

The human mind, body and achievement sequence is no different. In between the sensation of warmth and the action to flip on the fan, there is a process that takes the input from our sensors, processes it, and then decides what to do with that processed info. All the while this is happening beneath our conscious thinking.

By the time it gets to our conscious level, the heavy lifting has been done and all we (the conscious part of ourselves) just need to get up and complete the physical act.

There is one more similarity in the analogy of computer programs, and that is the use of a programing language. In typical programs, there are different languages used, and you've come across them, that tell the computer what to do. We humans have it too, and it is powerful. Like the invocation of the word "papa". When these words are used, they form the programming language that computers use in their algorithms. This is the study of NLP – Neuro Linguistic Programming. It is the use of ordinary words in a sequence to reach down and change the programing language of our nature towards actions that have benefits that carry us on the path to monumental and gargantuan success.

This is a beginner's perspective, but it is rather expansive and extensive, so buckle up. Words are everything in this day and age. We use words and sounds to convey specific things and actions and we can use those same words to stir up the energy to propel us. The problem is that some words can propel us in the direction opposite to the direction we intend or are prepared to traverse. We will cover that here as well.

The first step in understanding NLP is to understand that we all have diverse backgrounds and that background has had a significant impact on our programming language. In NLP, we empower our conscious mind to edit and alter that programming so that our habits, responses, and reactions are driven by a set of instructional algorithms that are geared toward extracting success from every situation, challenge, and opportunity.

The core of NLP is the understanding of behavioral mechanics. It is grounded in the study of behavioral sciences. Behavioral science concerns itself with the way the human mind absorbs input and processes it toward an output. All our actions are guided by our behavior. From the impetuous child crying on the toyshop floor to the kleptomaniac in custody for stealing, to the successful and hardworking student, and the highly accomplished statesman, we are all puppets of this algorithm that works beyond the sensory tentacles of our conscious mind.

While being a puppet may not necessarily sound appealing to many, it has its benefits and its uses. By relegating a number of tasks to the subconscious mind, and thereby conducting it on auto pilot, it leaves a large part of our conscious processing power to handle a number of other tasks.

Most people do not have the requisite faith to let their subconscious take control of a lot of what they do and that is because many suffer from faulty instincts and instinctive responses that have failed in the past. That is exactly what NLP will address and realign.

When you sit down to make a decision to move or abstain from something, there is a powerful current underneath your decision-making self that determines the outcome of that decision. Sometimes that underlying current is so strong that even if you use brute force to overcome it, it will sabotage you along the way, resulting in failure. The only way to overcome it would be to engage the strategies of NLP. NLP can reach into the processes that occur in the subconscious realm of your mind and unlock doors, tear down walls, obliterate barriers and move mountains when you strike the right tone.

At the heart of the NLP is the core of seeming silence that you need to access. We will show you how this is accomplished and the language that you can use and tailor to your particular circumstance.

Building on that, we explore the conscious mind and how it accomplishes its tasks. We also look at the subconscious or the preconscious mind and see what it takes to get that going. We also look at the areas of our life that the subconscious manages. Then finally, we have the conundrum of consciousness - something that many people confuse to mean a variation of the term conscious. It's not. It is much deeper and it is what makes us human. It is more than cognizance and more than sentience, it is a shadow of divinity and a projection of knowing. We will look at this briefly from a theoretical and functional perspective.

The underlying algorithm that controls the subconscious' propensity to act in one way or the other is a critical part of the entire NLP success. There is a distinctive structure that applies to each individual, and then there is an individual priority list that we need to determine. We will look at the elements of the algorithm and strategies of how to change what is needed.

The key element of NLP is something that is unexpected and it is the value of silence. This silence is not about inaction, or indecision, but rather is a language of its own. This language of silence is used extensively in NLP and we will introduce this concept and practice later on in the book.

With those basics, we will show you how to change your entire life around by tapping the subconscious with silence programming and language utilization. There are some exercises in here to get you comfortable with the different concepts and get you used to monitoring your program on the fly.

Introductory Exercise –

Changing the Content of Memories

We can't change the past for you, but we can show you how to alter the effects of it in this exercise. This is one of the major powers of NLP and you can dive right in to get underway with changes that you can use.

I've found that a good way to institute these changes is to be able to consciously do that at a certain time every day and then after a certain amount of time has passed they become a habit that you can rely on.

Exercise 0
1)   Set your timer to 90 seconds
2)   Get a piece of paper and divide it into three columns and label it as follows
i)   First Column – Person
ii)   Second Column – Feeling
iii)   Third Colum – Action
3)   When you are ready, start the timer and write as many people you know who come into your mind regardless of how those people make you feel. List them down using just their first name in the first column. Do this in rapid fire style and don't stop to linger on any single person or the memory associated with them.

4)   At the end of the timer, stop; don't fill out any more memories. This exercise is time sensitive.

5)   Put it aside and go about your day. You will not look at this list for the rest of the day (or night).

Exercise 0a

6)   On the following day come back to the list and start to fill out the second column.

7)   For each name in the first column write down how he/she makes you feel in the Feeling column.

8)   Use only one word to describe your feeling. Good, Bad, Angry, Sad, Disappointed, etc.

9)   When you are done, put that aside and don't look at it until the following day.

Exercise 0b

10)   On the third day, use a highlighter to mark off the words under the Feelings heading.

11)   Mark the words that are negative. For instance, let's say the Memory word in Column 1 is 'Tom', and the Feeling word in Column 2 is 'angry'. If you consider 'angry' to be a negative word, highlight it with your highlighter.

12)   When you are done, put that aside as well. Come back to it the following day.

Exercise 0c

13)   On the fourth day, it's time to put it all together and bring it home.

14)   Take the names of the people that you associate with negative feelings and change three things about yourself in front of them. The three things you change must come from three different sensory input categories. One for sight,

one for sound and one for touch. For instance, if Tom made you angry, think of yourself as a Minotaur (sight) that had arms like rocks (feel) and that growled loudly (sound) to the point it shrunk and shriveled Tom until he became this squeaky little mouse quaking in his paws... or something like that. The idea is to change yourself into something bigger, greater, and more powerful and alter your nemesis into something less significant thereby easily overcoming him in a mental match up.

15)   Do this every day for seven to fourteen days without once thinking ill of him (as opposed to thinking funny of him) but always thinking of yourself stronger and more powerful.

Doing this exercise is to get you to see how powerful your thoughts of your senses are and how you can alter things that have happened in the past.

Make short list of memories regardless of what they are using just one word to describe them. Use a timer and set it.

***

Chapter 1 Developments in Neuroscience

In the last three decades, we have made significant advances in the fields of neuroscience and psychology, allowing us better knowledge, understanding, and insight into the brain, the mind and the psyche of the human species, and living organisms in general. The interesting thing about these advances is that they are not just some esoteric discovery that impacts us from a distance. No. The advances have been significant, immediate and continue to directly impact every facet of our daily lives.

With advances in neuroscience, we have found that isolating disciplines of the brain only gets us so far, and then we hit a brick wall. We also instinctively know that there is more to the brain than just being a control center for internal bodily functions. It is also a tool to communicate and connect with the objects that occupy the environment around us.

Imagine a glass of water. Into this water, we add two color pigments: red and blue. Initially, you see them in three distinct layers, the red, the blue and the clear. In time the molecules of these pigments diffuse through the water and eventually you move from three distinct shades to one homogenous purple suspended in a matrix of water.

What the process of diffusion does to those pigments, our brain does for us by helping us assimilate the essence and information of our surrounding - it helps us to mingle, learn, take on other practices and homogenize our individuality. That is how we grow as individuals, and how we advance as a species.

We can't visually look at it, but what we know to be intangible thoughts and memories are actually physical connections that are made in the brain. The brain, and what goes on within it, is a juxtaposition of what is tangible in nature to what is intangible - look at it this way, holding your pen in your hand is tangible. Thinking and visualizing that same pen is intangible. There is another twist to it. What we just determined to be an intangible thought, memory, or vision, is actually caused by a physical, hence tangible, mental phenomenon. This phenomenon is the building of neural pathways. When a memory is formed, regardless of its origin, these strands are built. The more we are exposed to this experience, the stronger this fragment becomes, sometimes creating more than one neural pathway to the same outcome.

Thus the next step in true understanding is achieved by combining disciplines and looking at how the mind, brain, consciousness and the universe all work holistically. Neuropsychology is such a combination of disciplines, where we look at the structure of the brain, and the nature of the mind that is built on top of it. But that's theoretical, and as important as it is in the grand scheme of things, what flows from it is more important, and that is what lies at the core of our thesis in this book - Neuroplasticity.

The juxtaposition of neuroscience and psychology is of deep interest, as it has the potential to catapult our species forward at rates we can't even imagine and haven't yet seen. This area of neuroplasticity which is not exactly at its nascent stages is practical, functional and result oriented.

We consider neuroplasticity to be the focus of both the hard science of neuroscience and the soft science of psychology, because one influences the other, and vice versa. You can have neurons influence psychology and the way you think and act, and you can have the way you think and act influence the neural pathways. That is how our species is built - by mimicking. When we mimic a certain act, that builds a neural pathway and slowly, before long, the act we once mimicked becomes our own.

Neuroplasticity comes from the combination of two words, neuro, and plasticity. Neuro is something that we can fairly easily figure out and know that it has something to do with the brain, but plasticity is not something we come across very often. What it means is the malleability and flexibility - as something made of plastic would feel and look like, but more importantly behave like.

Essentially, neuroplasticity is the study of how the brain physically changes during one's lifetime to adapt to the circumstances it faces. The change can be structural - the recovery from a stroke, for instance; the change can be environmental - exposure to increased carbon monoxide; or it can be from ideological surroundings and cultural values. The physical brain constantly changes according to the forces it is subjected to, like plastic - thus the reference to plasticity. The brain's ability to respond to injury, stimuli and other parameters are no longer mere theory, they are verifiable proof.

There has been an increasing number of cases where patients who have suffered from mild to severe stroke were able to rehabilitate their condition and return to full upright biped mobility and ambidexterity because our brain is able to find alternate neural pathways to accomplish the connection between command and execution.

I mention this so that those of you who think that you are who you are, and that change is what you do to your clothes and hair, get to see that even in the extreme cases of strokes and injury, the brain can change. When you use NLP, and you use it even when you are new to its principles, you can slowly see your changes take hold. NLP has conclusively proven you can teach old dogs new tricks.

The Organic Brain

The fact that the brain is malleable is no longer in contention. Using this fact to rehabilitate injury, improve functionality, advance scope and possibly push the boundaries of what we know, is no longer wishful thinking but rather undeniable reality. That is the direction we will take with this book. We are not yet focusing on the medical or rehabilitative uses of NLP, but rather we are looking at using it to form the basis of creating a life that your conscious mind desires, be it success, wealth, health, happiness or just laid-back peace.

I want to bring NLP to you in a way that you can use in your everyday life and to improve any area that you need to, whether in school, friends, work, marriage, or wherever. I am confident that you can bring it together enough that the small changes you make with NLP result in big changes in your happiness. I've seen NLP work in a broad range of situations and across the lives of all it touches and the more I see it at work every day, the more I want to show you the possibility that you can alter, adjust, and shape your mind, your past and your future. This is the power of the gods because when you alter the shape of the mind, you are essentially changing your destiny.

Factors

You are born into this world with a certain set of attributes - from the geography of your birth to the geopolitical fortunes of your society. You are even subjected to environmental conditions and ideological pressures that mold you into who you are, but all those are mere forces, external to your internal being.

You must understand that you are the result of the sum of forces that act on you from the outside and the sum of forces that react to that environment from the inside. Mash-up ideology, beliefs and perception, and you get the makings of a life that is either suffering, indifferent, or suboptimal, but life can be more than that. It can be happiness and peace, depending on how you control your perception algorithm, and you can do that using NLP. If you reflect on your acts and observe the consequences, then we begin to understand the shape that a man's psyche begins to take. At the center of those forces are the brain and the human mind.

Time is a dimension you need to factor into all this. Those neural pathways forming in your head, with every experience you encounter, can be determined as a function of time. If a particular stimulus is repeated constantly, that causes stronger memory formation. Those pathways get stronger and last longer. When the stimuli cease, then the pathways atrophy over time –just like your muscles when you don't use them. In time, that neural pathway becomes inconsequential - something we refer to as 'forgetting'.

A Somewhat Deeper Philosophy

Three elements are at play in our existence - emptiness, substance, and time. All three are represented within the brain and its processes, and these are what mold the brain into what it is at any single point in time. This is essentially the field of neuropsychology and the basis of NLP.
One way to advance the effort to understand the workings of the psyche and the way NLP works, we need to look at how the brain works and how it is the foundation of the mind, and how the mind becomes the foundation for the psyche.

The physical melds into the intangible in a way that makes it difficult for us to always look at only one thing and not the other. The path this book takes is designed to gently hug the contours of the landscape and introduce the facts of the brain, the mind and the actions that flow from it in a functional way, and how it all also works in reverse. Thus it is important that we understand how the brain works from a cellular perspective and from a notional one.

Chapter One Exercise –

Reframing

The ability to reframe is not about being in denial about what is going on in your life. You are not changing what happened, but how you see what happened. The founders of NLP have stepped away from actively using this process and procedure, but it is still a very valid way of doing things and especially if you are doing it to yourself it works well. It takes some practice and when you do it often enough, long enough, you find that it is a great way to reflect. After all, you are consulting yourself and there is no better person that knows you better than you.

The exercise in the Introductory Chapter was a simple version of reframing; this one takes it a step further. The exercise is designed to reveal things about yourself to you. The first is that framing can be applied to almost everything you encounter, everything you perceive and everything that happens. One of the best movies I've ever watched, "Life is Beautiful" by Roberto Benigni, is exactly what reframing is about. If you haven't watched it, or it's been a while since you watched it, you should include it for movie night this week. Spoiler alert: Benigni plays a father and bookseller in a Nazi camp where he protects his son by giving him alternative interpretations of what is happening around them in an internment camp. He essentially reframed one of the most horrific events in history so that his son would not bear the scars of the event.

That's what reframing is about.

Exercise 1
Find an instance in your recent life where someone said something to you that really hurt you. Look back to that time, and what you are going to do is reframe the entire chain of events that led to that point where the verbal hurt was inflicted.

Once you find that chain of events, go back to a point in that chain and look at the things you did. Trust me, there were probably many. Look at the things you can control and look at the escalation that occurred. Now find a point somewhere in the early stages of that chain and reverse how you reacted to something. Reframe that one instance and see how the other person would have logically responded.

Only one of two things can result.

Either you realize that if you didn't contribute, things wouldn't have advanced to the point of hurt. Or you realize that no matter what you did, that person would have inflicted that pain on you, in which case, the person is not worth the emotion you have invested in it and thus he/she means nothing to you.

The moment you reframe the issue to either arrest control of all that transpired or reframe how much that person means to you, the final hurt that was inflicted evaporates.

Once you get the hang of reframing, you will be able to do it to almost anything you experience.

Chapter 2 Genesis, Apoptosis and Plasticity

Neuroplasticity is a fairly new area in the field of neuroscience and it is a key premise in NLP. It is based on the observation, as the name implies, that there is plasticity in the neurons that make up the brain. Neuroplasticity is not to be confused with neurogenesis - which is about the birth of new neurons. (Anything that uses the word 'Neuro" is probably concerned with the brain, and Genesis has to do with beginning – that should help you differentiate the terms)

Try to think of the brain in as simple terms as possible. The material here is not intended for you to become a neurosurgeon. You are only here for the functional understanding of how the mind works so that you can use it to advance your purpose and achievements.

To understand neuroplasticity, it would be a good idea to understand neurogenesis here and then lay the facts and science atop the former. It is also a good idea to understand neuroapoptosis and understand the stages and the lifespan of the neuron.

By understanding the life cycle, from birth to death, process of brain cells, we get to appreciate the power and the vulnerabilities of the brain and the mind that relies on it. We also get to appreciate the regenerative aspect of cell death. If the old cells don't die, new cells can't replace damaged cells. What a brilliant design.

While neurogenesis is possible and its existence is now verifiable, it is not without great effort and repetitive process of learning and therapy that a person who has lost their ability to walk or speak after an ischemic stroke has to endure.

Neurogenesis

As the name implies, genesis refers to the birth of something new. In this case, it is the birth of new neuron cells. It has been observed in recent research that there is a special stem cell that is responsible for the birth of new neurons and that they occur in a special part of the brain. The regeneration of new neuronal cells is a lifelong process, and in the event of new learning, new cells are formed on one part of the brain and then are moved to the location where it is needed.

In a way, neurogenesis is a subset of neuroplasticity from the perspective of, and only from the perspective of, adaptation after injury when exercised in a certain way.

In neurogenesis, the brain responds to stimuli when prompted by learning a new skill, or repeating a new skill, and forms a new neuron which it then moves from its place of birth, which is in the frontal cortex, to the place where it is needed. As such, in the event a stroke victim has damage in the area of the brain that is concerned with walking, assuming there is no other damage to the limb concerned and the ability to balance, then the process of neurogenesis creates new neurons and moves those neurons to the place in the brain that is appropriate for the ability to walk.

If the person is old, then the process takes a significantly longer time and the recovery is slow to take shape, and even after it does, the relearned skill of walking is not as smooth or stable as the pre-stroke ability.

The new neurons are born where the neuron stems cells are located. In an adult human being, that happens to be in the frontal cortex. Once the cell is born, it needs to be installed in the location where it is needed. As such, it needs to travel to that location.

There are two methods that the neurogenesis process uses to migrate the newly minted cell to its location. The first is the use of chemical signals. They are executed with the aid of Adhesion Molecules that are found on the new neuron and old neurons so that when they bind, they move along the old neuron until they get to the location that they need to be at. The second method is similar to the first, except this time they adhere to the radial glia, instead of the neurons themselves, and travel to their destination. Unlike previously hypothesized, neurons are not made on location, which is one of the reasons it takes time to learn new skills. When you do learn, it's always a good strategy to let the newly learnt knowledge sit for a while before attempting to use it.

It is interesting to note that only one in three new neurons arrives at their destination. Others get misplaced, and still, others experience premature apoptosis. The misplaced neurons cause more havoc in the brain as they have been studied and found to be the cause of schizophrenia in some adults and epilepsy in kids. Dyslexia is also a common side effect of misplaced neurons.

Expanding on where the neuron was intended to be placed, they will carry different functions. There is more than one kind of neuron. In fact, there are three. There is the motor neuron, the sensory neuron or an interneuron.

Motor neurons are responsible for carrying impulses from the brain through the spinal column to the muscle group that is in question. The sensory neuron does the exact opposite, it carries sensory information from the extremities and sensors back to the brain for processing.

Neuroapoptosis
Neuroapoptosis is the death of the neuronal cells in the brain and/or spinal column. Unlike the other cells in the rest of the body, which have comparatively short lifespans which range from a few days in the stomach lining to two weeks with skin cells and 120 days for blood cells; neuronal cells last almost the entire lifetime. The bulk of the cells are produced in the womb before delivery and then a little more after birth. So cell death is usually at the point when the body dies. This is in normal circumstances.

However, neuroapoptosis can also happen under the influence of alcohol, asphyxia and brain injuries as we have mentioned. The thing to note at this point is not about how cells die, but how they are replaced. Unlike most other cells, brain cells are not replaced when they die. They are only born when new cells are needed to do new tasks. If you consider this fact, it should start to dawn on you that the human body, the human mind, and there by the human condition has a design that makes it adaptable and limitless in ability. As Hamlet said, "What a piece of work is a man! How noble in reason, how infinite in faculty! In form and moving how express and admirable! In action how like an Angel! In apprehension how like a god! The beauty of the world! The paragon of animals! And yet to me, what is this quintessence of dust?"

How true, and with a little understanding of the brain, we can see why.

NLP and Neuroplasticity

Neurogenesis and neuroapoptosis are about the brain cells and its beginning, but neuroplasticity is about how neurons behave in their achievement of their purpose during their lifetime. Each neuron is connected to anywhere from a thousand to ten thousand other neurons, and there are about 100 billion neurons in total. That number stays fairly constant through a person's life unless certain steps are taken during the fetal developmental stage. It has long been lore that playing Mozart compositions for a fetus in the womb has this effect. For most of the children in a non-scientific study that was conducted where music was played for the full nine months of their pregnancy, it was observed (unscientifically) that the children who were

137

exposed to classical music (not just ones composed by Mozart) had a definite effect. Ten years later the same group of children was observed to have moved further in academics and social engagement than study subjects who were not exposed to prenatal music and stimulation.

A single neuron is not much of use when compared to that neuron connecting to thousands of other neurons. Their point of contact is called the synapse.

If you think about the brain, it is a physical, albeit a biological object. It is made up of live tissue, which is made up of no less than two different types of brain cells and is fed with oxygen and nutrient. The special thing about brain cells is that they are conductive in nature and they specifically transmit information electrochemically. Dendrites bring information to the cell, which travels down the axon and out via the axon terminals.

A neuron in isolation only has one use - it holds a fragment of information in isolation. This is overcome when the neuron connects with another neuron that has another piece of information. In this same way, each neuron connects to thousands of other neurons, but that connection is not a physical one. There is a gap. This is ingenious actually. If the connection was seamless, then there will just be information flowing all over the place, and from a practical perspective, that would mean a lot of the information would physically collide with one another and become vastly incoherent and thus useless.

Instead, there is a gap between the neurons, specifically between the synapses. This gap acts as a boundary between one neuron and the next, and in that gap, neurotransmitters are used to go from one neuron to the next.

When an electrical impulse moves from the Soma through the Axon and down to the terminus, it sparks the release of vesicles that contain the neurotransmitters. These neurotransmitters then leave the axon terminus and jump the gap into the attached neuron. That neuron could be attached by the dendrite, the axon or the terminus of another neuron. Depending on where one neuron attached to another, it gives rise to specific term - axodendritic synapse, axoaxonic synapse, and axosomatic synapse. Obviously, the first terms are where the axon terminus is attached to the dendrites, the second is attached to the axon and the final one is where it is attached to the soma.

Take Away
The thing that you need to take away from all this is that NLP is based on solid science and verifiable understanding of neuropsychology. The actual exercises that you undertake at the end of this chapter, and all the other chapters are simple, yet they will impact how you think and how you react to things that happen to you. The time when this is hardest to execute is in the face of pain, but even pain is a concept that you can change. If you get into the habit of watching workout videos on YouTube, you will notice,

aside from the chiseled bodies on display, that they have a very different definition of pain than you. They have redefined pain, albeit physical pain.

***

Chapter Two Exercise –

Seven Day Rebirth

This is a very simple exercise. I want you to make a list of things that you would like to change in yourself. These are perhaps little habits – we shall start small and work our way up. For instance, if you have a spending problem, I don't want you to change your spending habit overnight, but what I want you to do instead is to get a little book, and in it, I want you to write down every single cent that you spend, when you spend it. If you have a problem with profanity, I want you to write down when and where and with whom you were when you cussed. It has to be done right there when it happens. Taking out that little book and pen and writing down whatever habit you want to get rid of every time you do it is merely a physical manifestation of being accountable for your actions.

That's all I want you to do, and I want you to do it for seven straight days, EVERY time it happens. Let's not tackle things like smoking or alcohol, remember BABY STEPS. If you forget, I want you to start all over again and do it for seven days. Even if you are on the evening of the sixth day and you break it, you have to start again.
That's it. That's all you have to do.

***

Chapter 3 Brain Power

It should be obvious by now that for any of the things we have spoken about up to this point would be moot if the specific neuron or group of neurons were not functioning or effectively dead. It is possible to have thousands of neurons in the space of a red bean since each neuron can measure between 4 and 100 microns. These neurons are supplied with a rich supply of oxygen and nutrients because the activities of the neurons take up tremendous energy. In the event there is an injury and the affected area consists of parts of hundreds of neurons, the body would have to find a way of repairing it.

There are two ways of repairing it - one direct and the other indirect. In the indirect method, whatever skill or memory that is lost with the death of that group of neurons can be re-learnt, and in that event it is possible that with significant effort expended, the brain creates new neurons and sends it to this area. But this is not a direct replacement. The new neuron would go to the area of the old neuron, but it would not have the same connections that the old neuron had. The new neuron would have to make up the connections that the old neuron had and that would take a lot of effort and time, but the important thing is that it can be done.

The second method utilizes neuroplasticity. In the event of minor damage or in the event of minor degradation, the brain, instead of creating new neurons, makes use of the old one by just forming new connections in different locations. If there were four neurons, for instance, A, B, C, and D. And in this example A connects to B, which connects to C. D is not connected to anything here but to other neurons and is a replica of B. In the event B were to become defective or die, then the crux of neuroplasticity would be that A and C now form new synaptic connections to D.

It is also possible that entire neurons don't get damaged. The only part that does get damaged is maybe a dendrite or two and possibly one of the axon terminals. In this case, it is possible to lose a connection with another neuron and so no dendrites grow to make a new connection. This is a form of neuroplasticity.

The whole point of neuroplasticity is to be able to keep thoughts and functions in the brain intact in the event of two things. One, in the event that there is damage to the neuron; and second, in the event, you want to change an ingrained habit and override something that you have already learned. A good way to do this is to erase past connections and create new ones. This is the whole point of neuroplasticity, and now you see how you are able to change old habits, like the one you were exercising in the last chapter's exercise.

But the first step to any habit change is to acknowledge significantly, two aspects of the habit. The first is to acknowledge that it is a habit you want to be free from. You did that the moment you wrote down which habit you wanted to drop.

The second is to acknowledge each time the habit kicked in. You did that each time you wrote down the habit when you acted it out. Acknowledging a habit makes your brain realize (as opposed to just knowing) that it is doing something it shouldn't. It also realizes which neurons it needs to erase and make new neurons to circumvent the neurons that cause the habit. Don't worry about the technical part, just do the exercise. At the end of this chapter, you will revisit the outcome of the previous exercise and you will be able to do something about it.

The Most Powerful Feature of the Brain

The entire point of this book on NLP is to show you the science and the practice of how you can change your lot in life. You have the power and the responsibility to change, but it can be tough. I get that. I've been there, and I still am. The only time we are not 'there' is when we are perfect, and I can tell you none of us are perfect.

We have traveled across multi disciplines to get to this specific point - how to change your brain so that you can become a new person – a person better than the one you were yesterday and significantly better than the one you were a year, or even a decade ago. But within NLP is hope, because if you can change who you are today and make yourself incrementally better than you were yesterday, you can make yourself better than you are today when tomorrow comes.

When you understand neuroplasticity, neuropsychology, and the practical aspects of NLP, what should be apparent, and what should dawn on you, is that you can be whoever you want to be because everything you are boils down to connections of synapses and the chain-linking of neurons. And because of the new science of neuroplasticity, we are now able to conclusively determine that it is entirely possible to change who we are from thoughts to mindsets to behaviors and actions. All of which are literally anchored in the chains of neurons and its liked synaptic connections.

All the physical processes we saw above are real. The key addition to this picture that we need to consider is that most of our actions are initiated by a subconscious process, and converted into conscious desire. If you already want it, but haven't got it, or haven't done it, it doesn't matter. Sometimes, just acknowledging what you want gets you half way there.

When you ask for help, pray for guidance, wish for health, you are merely consciously acknowledging what your subconscious has already figured needs to happen.

However, we, as conscious beings, also want a say in what we want to become and how we want to be. There are still some aspects of the present that the subconscious is not able to handle entirely on its own because of its long standing links to historical and evolutionary forces.

For instance, one such archaic force is the fight, flight or freeze response. We no longer are hunted by animals whose eyesight is primarily driven by movement. During times that we were, the freeze response would be of aid in helping us hide from visual detection and from attracting the attention of the predator. We would also be able to play dead. Predators do not like dead prey, so they move on. But we no longer face that situation anymore. So the fight, flight and freeze response does not need the freeze aspect of it, and that is where the conscious brain comes in and tells us that we shouldn't freeze, and this desire to not do so slowly changes our brain in the process we have just learned to call neuroplasticity.

It turns out we can control this neuroplasticity. All we need is the awareness of possibility and the will to repeat the steps needed to get it done. In the Exercise chapter, we will lay out the steps you need to choose what you want to change in your life, then get your brain in the mode that promotes neuroplasticity. It will take anywhere from 8 weeks to start to see the difference in your life.

***

Chapter Three Exercise –

Change What Needs Changing

We see that the most important and the most powerful ability of the brain is to be able to change in a way that affords you the mobility to adapt, yet gives you the anchor to habitualize. You just need to have the wisdom to be able to apply the right skill to the right task.

You created habits because of a system of punishment and rewards in your physiology. When you have the habit to do something, and the trigger creates the need for the habit to take over, your body applies the stick to you in the form of discomfort. When you perform the act, the discomfort ceases and instead you are rewarded. That, not only ensures that you conduct the act, but strengthens it so that you will fall in line quicker the next time. You can use that to your conscious advantage. This exercise will show you how.

Exercise 3
Dig up the book that you listed all the things you wanted to change from the last exercise. Go over it and look at how you did it and how often you

did it. Let that sink in and ask yourself why you do it and what real gain do you get from it. Does there seem to be any logic to it? If there is logic to it, what is it? How does it benefit you? If it doesn't, why do you do it? Its habit, isn't it?

To change the habit all you need to do is decide that you do not need it anymore in your life and the exercise that you need to perform is to find an exact opposite habit to replace it with. A good exercise would be to replace profanity with a similar sounding word that is innocuous. When you do that, you get the reward of saying the word where the sound is close enough that you get the reward of the habit but don't get the demerit on your character.

So for instance, if you keep using the word " sh*t" you change it to "Shoot". If you like the "F**K" word, change it to "freak". Baby Steps, remember?

Do this for seven days. Without fail, if you slip, restart the clock.

***

Chapter 4 Steps to New Life

You can't just jump in and start messing with the neural connections and the synapses in your brain. If you do it this way, you would probably not have any success, and in fact, you may even be damaging what you already have. As with anything, the first thing you need to do is understand the awesome power that is at your hands with what you are about to do here. The second thing is that you have to create the willpower to do the steps that you need to do to get to where you want to go and who you want to be.

The third is that you need to believe that what you are about to embark upon does have significant benefit for you, more so than what you have right now. The one thing that your subconscious is good at is calculating cost to benefit ratios, and it knows that if you are about to embark on something that is less worthy compared to what you already have, you will find your subconscious trying to sabotage you internally. It is one of the reasons many people fail at trying to elevate themselves - because they do not believe in what they are doing and they do not have the facts to prove it to themselves. The currency between your conscious and your subconscious is desire and belief. If you have sufficient amounts of those, your subconscious will be on board.

With those three elements in our understanding, it is time to layout the steps you need to accomplish to become a new person - someone who you choose to be.

Reflection

Your first step is sincere and deep reflection. This is what you do to change the neurons in your head by working on the things that matter to you. If you are the intellectual type, then you need to think your way through it. If you are the physical type, then you need to alter your thoughts by doing something physical to change the way your mind would act for a particular area – the old folks at home used to call these sorts of acts to alter paths, rituals. I am not one for mumbo jumbo, but there is no mumbo jumbo in performing rituals to alter the mind, and you will be surprised how well this works at changing things.

When you do deep reflection, you are probing your conscious and using logic to decipher your subconscious. When you want to change what you find, and you act in accordance to that, your neurons that represent that thing you want changed, begin to alter. It's connections change, and pretty soon something takes its place. Identifying neurons, the pathways that those neurons form and the bunch of networks that all point to the area that you want to change can be replaced by the neurons that represent your desire. It's like making a wish and blowing a candle. The wish is silent and the blowing of the candle is the action. Together, the ritual gets you what you want. I don't know about you, but I remember getting every one of those things I wished for. Sure, I had to work for it, but I was under no delusion that it would appear out of thin air.

Of course, you will not be cognizant of where those neurons are and what they look like. Your brain takes care of that for you. All you have to do is think about the areas in your life that you need to change and the areas in your life that you are looking at that need to be improved.

In the last two exercises of your habit acknowledgment, you approached it two steps. Can you guess which step is more important than the other? Yup, the part that you took the time to be aware of your habit or thing that you wanted to change is the more important element of the two. In that one week of constantly writing it down, what you did was become aware at a cerebral level, and the mind looked at itself and said, "Ok I now know where to go to get that changed."

NLP and Reflection
Reflection doesn't require any special skill except the honesty and the ability to trace your steps from the things that you have been responsible for to the lot in life you currently experience. The first character of a person who will be successful in reflection is the person that will be brutally honest with himself and a person who will take responsibility for all the things that happen to him and the causes of those things. You see, without taking responsibility for something, you will not be able to control it in the future, and if you do not control that element in the future, you will not be able to change your lot in life.

The moment you start with reflection and you start telling yourself that you are going to, from this day forth, take responsibility for your actions, you would have already started the changes in the neural pathways that govern your outlook on life and luck.

After repeatedly telling yourself this, you will find that it will start to become your reality and you will be able to reach deeper into your reflection to find the areas that you need to identify that will give you the life that you are in search of.

If you think you want a new BMW. You know what, you're probably going to be able to get it if you engage in this, but why would you want to stop at something so pedestrian and inconsequential. Do you think Steve Jobs wished that he bought a new Mercedes?

No, he wished to be the instrument that changed the world, and his pathways evolved and he did change the world, the convertible Mercedes he did eventually buy was secondary.

In the process of reflection, the first step is to understand what you want. The second step is to find out what part of you is blocking you from getting there. That will help you to find where you are at the moment. You are essentially trying to plot a map that shows where you are and where you want to go. This, and the desire to take responsibility for your life, will begin to get the process of neuroplasticity working in your favor. Desire and belief, as we said, are the two things that you need to get yourself in the game.

Asking

Your second step is the process of asking. When you ask, and you ask repeatedly, your subconscious starts the force of taking all the things you know, whether you are aware of it or not, and it starts to plot a path to where you need to be. Asking is a powerful tool and you should never discount the act of asking. If you are too shy to ask, that is a sure sign that you either feel that you don't deserve it, or you are too arrogant to ask for it. Both of those characteristics will trip you up and mess with your ability to alter the neurons that will put you in the frame of achievement. When you ask, it also helps to ask that you become the person that can achieve what you are looking for, not just asking for the thing that you want.

Meditation

The final step in your neuroplasticity process is to meditate. Meditation has proven to place your brain in such perfect state in the frequencies that it needs, that neuroplasticity is promoted aggressively in various state of meditation. Sleep does the same thing if you do it right. In most mainstream NLP programs, meditation has not been stressed on. But there are some strong NLP programs that look at a very specific strain of meditation to advance the changes in cognitive ability and in character alteration.

In the same way that meditation can be of aid, focused sleep can do the same thing. But you will have to do it in a certain way, different from what you are typically used to. First of all, you need to tire yourself out with a very high level of work in the day. This means that you work out and get the necessary neurotransmitters pumping. With vigorous workout, you will get your body to release the right hormones that will promote deep sleep.

Before you sleep, conduct your reflection, your asking, and your meditation. Make sure you keep your meditation focused and not blank. There are two kinds of meditation. One is to keep your mind absolutely blank and let your subconscious take over.

The other kind of meditation is to increase your brain's conscious capacity and concentrating intently on just one thing, in this case, concentrate on the thing that you are asking for. Do not fantasize.

When you desire, believe, ask and meditate, you set up the necessary elements for your brain to change the way it is to become the way it needs to be to give you what you desire. No other method can effect faster and longer lasting change than following the three steps that are simple.

But there is one impediment to this that most people are not aware of. If in the process of reflecting and asking, if you are confused over what you want, your brain is not going to allow any changes to its existing pathways. It is the way nature protects us from flighty and transient fancies. You have to ask for something that you really want and it is a long term change that you are making. If you want short term changes, then you should look at changing your habits, but if you want long term changes, and that would mean that you want to change the way you see success, or the way you work out, or the way you acquire knowledge, then you attack the brain with the tools you have learned here.

It is important that you understand the way your mind works and the way neuroplasticity works with the different parts of your mental processes. You can see discernable changes after you consistently practice the three steps above over the course of at least eight weeks.

This has not been a course in neuroscience, or psychology. Rather it has been a book that shows you the rationalization of a simple process that will help you determine the course of the rest of your life.

You need to understand the basics of the brain's workings so that you can absorb the sea of data and columns of commentary out there explaining everything from the basics of neurogenesis, to neuroplasticity, and be able to sift through what is plausible from what is bunk.

But if you want to put aside all the scientific jargon and just drill down to the actionable intelligence that is contained amidst the lines of this book, then you need to focus on just three things.

First, you need to be able to reflect honestly and without interruption. Reflection, even though it seems to be thrown about aimlessly in today's metaphysical industry, holds a very powerful part of the human evolution and the story of our development. There is no doubt that each of us is trying to be better at one thing or another. That would be true in your case as well, if not, why else would you be here within these lines.

If you can't see why reflection is important to the growth of your psychological self and your material gain in this world, think about the analogy of the map. If you had no idea where you are, I could give you the most detailed 3-D map and the location of the world's largest trove of precious treasure, and you would have no way of getting to it if you did not know where you were. That is exactly what reflection does.

It seeks to alert your consciousness to things your subconscious already knows. But you need to alert your conscious mind because it is your conscious mind that is making the decision to go on the quest for that treasure. In your case, the treasure happens to be the most powerful thing known to man, and that is the ability to get whatever he truly desires.

To be successful and to attain what your heart desires, you must have a certain mindset that will allow you to make all the right moves in response to each situation and stimuli. How you react to something is just as important as how you act in the absence of external stimuli. This pattern of reaction, and this mindset of responses, are all neatly mapped out in your neural pathways.

But not everything that is mapped out is something that you did or that you wanted.

Sometimes it was just environmental forces that forced you to react in a certain way, and that reaction took hold of how you do things. But upon reflection, you realize that needs to be changed. Or, in another way, you could have been involved in a horrific experience that changed the way you see things or the way you respond to things and that, too, is a function of the neurological pathways that developed. To shake off those chains, you need to know that those pathways can be altered or even erased, given sufficient time and effort. Because the brain is designed to evolve and cope, it has a process of neuroplasticity and it allows you to alter the echoes of the past so that you can determine the beat of your future.

To change your life you have to want it. The brain responds to desire and belief. If you desire something, it means that that which you desire is already yours, you just have to work at getting it, and one of the first things you need to do is have the mindset that you can do everything and anything that it takes to get it done.

When you want it bad enough, the pathways of your brain begin to alter to the point that it needs to be able to put you within striking distance of what you need. Once you reflect and you begin to understand your strengths and weaknesses, you will be able to curb your weakness and fortify your strength from a neurological perspective.

Once you have reflected, then the process of asking repeatedly for that which you want and desire goes on to fortify those neurons and the connections that it needs to make. Each path is strengthened and each path is bolstered with redundant neurons to make sure that, in the case of injury, you are left with an alternate neurological path to your objective. You will find that the things most important to you are not easy to forget, but the things that are not can be fairly easy forgotten.

If you were to draw an analogy of creating your dreams and forging a sword, the first two steps of reflecting and asking would be like the steps of shaping the steel and hammering it. When you want to really make that sword strong, you still have one more step to do, you have to fire it in the furnace. You need to subject it to a force that brings it together and casts it in a way that it is unshakeable and unbreakable.

This is what meditation does. Meditation has been repeatedly proven to alter and redraw the lines of the pathways and get you to the point of renewing yourself from who you were to who you want to be. Being in a constant state of meditation is a great way to sharpen your focus and operate at a highly effective and efficient level.

***

Chapter Four Exercise –

Association and Desire

The point of Chapter 4 was to get you acquainted with ways your mind can understand your subconscious better and how your mind (the conscious part of it) can effectively communicate with your more powerful subconscious mind. To understand the dynamics of the two parts of your mind, think of them as the wheels that steer and the wheels that drive. The metaphor is limited, but it serves its purpose here. The subconscious is akin to the wheels that drive. It is where the power is. The conscious mind is akin to the wheels that steer – it gives you direction. Together you get to where you want to go in an efficient way.

For this chapter, we want to try to connect the conscious and the subconscious so that you are more efficient in where you want to go. To be able to do this you will need to understand what your desires are and how you associate with them.

Exercise 4
1)   Use a large sheet and divide it into three columns
a)   The first column should contain the label "Desire"
b)   The second column should be labeled "Reason"
c)   The third column should be labeled "1 – 100"

2)   Make a list of all the things you wish you had in your life using one word and place that in the first column. Give yourself 60 seconds. Finish column one before going on to column two.

3)   In the second column write down the reason you want that thing in your life. For instance, if you desire a Ferrari, and you place that in the first column, write down what that Ferrari means to you. Complete the first column from top to bottom before doing the second. For instance, on my list, I have the Lightning LS218 as something I wish to have. It is a desire of mine. The LS218, for those who don't know, is a Superbike, but it's not just any superbike, this one does over 200mph and is driven purely by electricity. Under the 'reason' column, I wrote, without realizing it – 'different'. Apparently to me, upon deeper reflection, I realize that I have always been someone outside the norm of tastes. The electric bike is different, and it is not something that is widely accepted. The desire of that bike was a clue in helping me understand what my true desires were. The bike just represents the desire, but if you can find the reason behind that desire; you can satisfy it better than just a product that may fizzle soon after. Your desires are clues.

Chapter 5 Focus and Observation

Staying in the moment requires the discipline to not be distracted. The discipline to remain in the moment comes from a simple decision that is then repeatedly practiced and reinforced.

The Brain

The brain is an amazing organ. If you think about it, the brain is able to form the nexus between the physical world and the incorporeal. Scientists, who have come so far in understanding the brain, admit there is still so much they can't explain. Recent studies by Prof Roger Penrose, a colleague of Prof Stephen Hawking, has even done experiments to conclude that some parts of the brain operate on quantum mechanics, which means that within this feeble body of ours, sitting within a delicate brain, is a device that can communicate at quantum levels.

It's needless to say that we use a very small portion of our brain to accomplish comparatively mundane tasks of talking, walking, eating, and even foraging. Of course, those tasks keep us alive, and as mundane as they may be, are a necessary list that needs to be taken care of, but our brain is capable of so much more. It is our mind that can get in the way.

The fortunate thing is that that we can literally change our mind because the mind is built on the faculties of the brain. The brain is the physical object that has physical characteristics. It has tissue, vessels, neurons, and synapses. It is limited by physical conditions of the body. It is affected by what you eat and what you breath - physical considerations.

The Mind

The mind, on the other hand, is incorporeal. You can't find it physically, yet it pervades all of your brain, and it is affected by genetic dispositions via the brain. After conception, while in the womb, the brain begins to take shape, and soon after that, the mind starts its assembly.

The brain and mind come together to bridge the phenomenal aspect of our universe and the noumenal aspect of our existence. Because of this, it becomes tricky when we want to explain the concept of observation and focus in any real fashion. Most explanations are cursory in nature and only serve generic use, but we want to deal in the truth of the matter and lay out the real issue of observation and focus, and what you will find is that it is related to being aware and living in the present moment.

Focus and observation are two very different things. Each requires the brain if they are to manifest, yet they are part of the parameters defined by the mind. To prove that focus, an intangible act is grounded in the tangible brain, look at the relationship between certain medications that can impair or enhance brain functions and then be visually observed in the person's actions. Even alcohol has that effect.

Focus and Observation

To say we focus on an event means that we open a channel to that event and we assimilate all that it has to offer. Imagine a physical conduit that is impermeable to external seepage. In that condition, the flow from the object to the mind is absolute with no distractions. That is absolute focus. The mind and the object become one by virtue of this conduit. However, from a functional standpoint, the mind will never allow itself to be 100% focused on an object to the point that the mind affixes itself to the object. This is because the fear center of the brain will preclude the brain from being closed to possible incoming alerts. Imagine being in a situation where you are at total focus, meaning you are fully attached to something. If anything emergent occurred during that session, you would not be able to extract yourself and attend to that emergent event. Absolute anything is never good, even when it is absolute focus.

The fear center of the brain is always on alert for events that could cause harm; the only thing that differs from one person to the next is the level and intensity of the focus.

You can also think about focus and observation (which are two very different things) in the following terms. We saw earlier how we analogized focus by attaching a conduit from the person to the object. The more permeable the conduit it is the less focused the person is on the event. Because permeability suggests that other

165

things external to the conduit can penetrate the flow in the conduit, when you use this analogy, the observation is the qualitative description for the amount of data that is received by the receiver. A person who is more focused can observe more than a person who is less focused.

The mind has a component to it that makes it one of the strongest tools any living animal has - we have the power to imagine - which is the power to make up things that are not in existence. But this power can sometimes work against us. It works against us by filling gaps of what we haven't fully observed. In some cases, we call this assumption, but this is more. When the mind does not fully capture an event it is observing, it fills in the blanks with assumptions based on experience. The end observation is inaccurate. Ceteris paribus, the lower the level of concentration the lower level of actual information capture, resulting in a higher level of assumption and the lower level of accuracy.

The reverse is true as well. The better the person's focus is, the higher the integrity of the conduit joining the event and the observer, and the higher the data being streamed. This makes the observation more accurate. In other words, the more one focuses, the more one observes, and the closer and faster to the truth one approaches.

One of the ways to make this work for you is to consciously apply NLP techniques to understand and change areas of your thinking to be able to overcome fear and resistance.

The point of NLP that no one really talks about is because it is becoming quite an industry. Most of you don't really need a coach, and if you do, it's probably toward the more advanced stuff. You don't always need a coach to accomplish the things that are in your own head. This isn't psychotherapy. The real reason you need coaches is that they seem to ask the right questions. The only thing you need to do is ask yourself the right questions and you will find that the answers await you.

Chapter Five Exercise –

Putting it Together

Your ability to arrange your life and get what you want out of it, whether it's peace at home, friends at work, or even the promotion, is not dependent on anyone in this world. It doesn't depend on your parents or the neighborhood you were born in. It does not depend on your town or the friends you knew. It doesn't depend on your spouse or kids. It depends only on you because of one simple fact, and that is the list of filters you apply to everything that touches your five senses.

You have a strong understanding of the brain, the mind and the ability to change anything you need to. The one thing that you now need to understand is the secret to changing things so that you can supercharge your abilities.

Here are five principles you need to remember and apply to your daily life:

1)   You can change anything with sufficient effort and repetition.
2)   All big changes come in incremental changes that you focus on one moment at a time.
3)   You can change anything in the universe if you are willing and able to alter your perception and reaction.
4)   How you associate something to your core beliefs will determine how you succeed.

5)   The words you use in your daily conversations will influence the trajectory of your life.

Exercise 5
1)   Make a list of all the things you want to achieve. This list must be on a sheet with three columns. The three columns are labeled as follows:
a)   Achievement
b)   Reason
c)   Importance (1 – 100)
2)   Put a clock on the exercise and do the list in 20 seconds.
3)   Put all the things you want to achieve in the first column and write as many as you want.
4)   Next, go to column two and use one word to describe the reason why you want to achieve it.

5)   When you're done with the second column, go to the third column and score it with a number from 1 – 100. 100 being the state you are most psyched about.

Once you've done this, you can put this list aside and reflect on what all this means. When you do this in rapid fire, you will be able to dig up what you really feel and you will be able to use the logic of your mind to ponder and reflect on it. Once you have this list, fold it and keep it in your pocket and look back at it whenever you can and make adjustments if you think you need to. But the one thing that you want to do is be aware of the contents.

Exercise 6

1) Look at the desires that you scored the lowest and tackle that one first.

2) Draw a map that takes you from where you are now to where you will achieve that achievement.

3) Break down the steps you need to get to from where you are to where you want to be. Make sure they are incremental steps. Never try to leap over anything that you can do in baby steps.

Exercise 7

1) Go back to the list you did in Exercise 5.

2) Look at all the steps that you outlined to get to where you want to get to and look at what part of you is blocking the achievement of that baby step. Find the 'neuron' in you that is stumbling the effort in the past and find a way to build a neuron around it. You do that by association and by replacement. If you have to do a ritual for it, go for it. Whatever it is, identify the offending step and get around it.

3) Legitimize your fears for each baby step and diminish those fears with action and understanding.

4) Put in the effort and get the direction. Spin your subconscious mind and turn your conscious mind toward your goals by aligning them and unifying your purpose.

5) Finally, remove all negative words, associations, and concepts from your lists and vocabulary. If you can't do something, and you can't change yourself to work toward that

something, change that something and look for the reason you went after it in the first place and find a substitute that will satisfy the reason.

***

Conclusion

Neuro Linguistic Programming is a hugely successful program because it resonates with a wide swath of thinking and behavior patterns. It will, no doubt, have an impact on you. To what degree that impact is, depends on how far you pursue it and how receptive you are to 'just another self-help program'.

Let me tell you that this is a very simple program at the early stages and can get daunting especially for some of us who are really wired differently and find that psychobabble is not real. That's the main reason I included the science behind the brain. The evidence for the scientific facts of the brain, neuroplasticity and how you are who you are is incontrovertible.

Your beliefs are something that you don't realize and you should take the time to take stock of them. There might be something that is tripping you up that you don't fully comprehend. It could be a simple matter and easily fixed, but because you are not aware of it, it is tripping you up.

I had a very close friend who had spent the last eleven years failing at every business he touched. He was like the anti-Midas. His family had stuck by him and he was a gem of a guy. All of us who were friends with him felt the pain and didn't know how to help. He came to work for me in the spring of 2015 and I entrusted him with a major project we were working on. Within six months of getting on the job, he had outlined the entire transaction and it was brilliantly done. He was really good at what he did and that made it even more intriguing why failure seemed to haunt him at every step.

Then I witnessed it in living color.

The morning of the final negotiation, as I sat there, he killed the deal. The clients left in short order and no one from our side could figure what was happening. Two weeks later, I took him to a friend of mine who has a hypnosis clinic and after only the third session in as many days, we found out from him, while he was under, that he and his father had a serious argument years ago. Jason (not his real name for obvious reasons) loved his father to a fault, but he was caught in an unfortunate series of events that required he marry his college sweetheart. He finished college but his father didn't want him to marry her but instead get his career on track first. The day he made the decision to marry, his father told him he would be a total failure by the time his child turned five.

His son had just turned 16 the week before the hypnosis, and we calculated that his failures for the last eleven years dated back to about the time his son turned five.

Coincidence? Hardly.

Words have meaning. More than we realize or care to admit.

It was obvious his father didn't mean it literally, but words, sound, and language have a way of penetrating our psyche and moving us in ways we don't really understand or fathom. What happened to Jason was no one's fault. Jason went through significant NLP and hypnosis therapy for six months and has catapulted to success beyond words.

We are all like Jason in many ways. We are bombarded by words, sounds, interpretations and all manner of distractions disguised in ways we don't realize or recognize. It is up to us to keep track of what has penetrated our psyche and what is affecting us. You've taken the first step to do just that. Congratulations. I trust you will find what you are searching for because all you need to do is get underway, as you have. Your brain will figure the rest out.

If you enjoyed learning about Hypnosis and NLP, I would be forever grateful if you could leave a review on Amazon. Reviews are the best way to help your fellow reading find the book worth reading so make sure to help them out!

Made in United States
Troutdale, OR
04/28/2024

19500087R00108